MY IMPOSSIBLE DREAM

By Chuck Randall

Hall of Fame Basketball Coach
and
Inventor of the Slam-Dunk Rim

as told to Barbara Kindness

BOOK PUBLISHERS NETWORK

Book Publishers Network
P.O. Box 2256
Bothell • WA • 98041
PH • 425-483-3040

10 9 8 7 6 5 4 3 2 1

Printed in the United States of America

LCCN 2007942455
ISBN10 1-887542-67-1 Hard cover
        1-887542-68-X Soft Cover
ISBN13 978-1-887542-67-8 Hard cover
        978-1-887542-68-5 Soft cover

A portion of the proceeds from the sale of this book will go into the Chuck Randall Endowment in the Western Washington University Foundation.

Editor Proofreader: Julie Scandora
Cover Design: Laura Zugzda
Typographer: Stephanie Martindale

DEDICATION

This book is dedicated to my lovely wife and family who, I discovered, are more important than basketball.

Contents

PROLOGUE

It seems like every day we read in the newspaper or hear on the radio about some poor senior citizen's being taken advantage of. Often, it's a physical assault – a little old lady has her purse snatched as she walks down the street; or an elderly couple gets mugged while on vacation in unfamiliar surroundings.

But even more tragic, I believe, are the dozens of ways the elderly get scammed without even realizing it at the time. Life savings have been lost, property stolen, human dignity trampled on. Seniors born in the early twentieth century grew up in an era when you could trust your friends, neighbors, and especially your relatives. When a "helping hand" was just that, with no expectation of reciprocity. When the golden rule (do unto others as you would have them do unto you) was learned in early childhood. They were taught to be honest and forthright, so it was inconceivable that anyone – unless he or she were an outlaw – would deliberately act otherwise.

A few summers ago, I was tending my booth at the King County fairgrounds, trying to interest passers-by in my first very own invention, a Christmas Tree Toter. It was a blistering hot day, somewhat of a rarity in the Puget Sound region. I was wilting fast when one David Rainney strolled by, paused at my booth, and asked me about the product. He proceeded to tell me about a friend of his – Chuck Randall – who was also an inventor; in fact, he had invented the breakaway rim that had changed the sport of basketball, both on the collegiate and professional level. I didn't know much about the sport but soon learned that Chuck was in the Hall of Fame and had even been named Coach of the Century at Western Washington University.

I was still only somewhat interested, but then David said he thought that it was such a shame that Chuck had gotten scammed out of the royalties from this great invention. That got my attention! How dare someone cheat a fellow-inventor out of his profits! I gave my card to David and said I wanted to meet this Chuck Randall so I could perhaps help him. I found the crime even more despicable because it was perpetrated by a trusted professional.

A week later, Chuck called, and I drove up to visit him at his home near Bellingham. What I discovered was the most humble, unassuming man I had ever met. His basement workshop was a clutter of various materials he had collected to work on other inventions, along with a prototype of the Slam-Dunk Rim and memorabilia from many years.

By the time I left several hours later, I was convinced that Chuck's story should be told, not just the story of the Slam-Dunk Rim but also his fascinating journey and the many young lives he influenced along the way. We agreed that a portion of the proceeds from the sale of this book would go into the Chuck Randall Endowment in the Western Washington University Foundation. Up until now, the funds have gone to the men's program, but this will provide much-needed scholarships for the women's basketball program at Western Washington University.

Rose Brittain

ACKNOWLEDGEMENTS

Hundreds and hundreds of people have crossed my path throughout my eight-plus decades, and they've all played some role in enriching my life experience. From elementary school playground teachers to college basketball coaching peers; from a wonderful wife and children to a skillful hospital staff who kept me alive; from countless friends, players, fellow churchgoers, bridge-mates, and golf-mates – all are too numerous to mention by name and I would surely forget someone. In recent years, I have become an insatiable reader, and so, too, I feel a real kinship with such writers as Dr. Wayne Dyer.

But most of all, I want to acknowledge my "head coach," God, who has guided me through triumph and trial. Before each game, in our locker room, I asked my players to all gather in a circle, on our knees and holding hands, where we would recite the following prayer. It gave a sense of unity and commitment that stayed with us all, long after the final buzzer. That prayer tradition had begun years before when former Harlem Globetrotter Don Barnette came to our basketball camp and taught it to us.

Chuck

The Athlete's Prayer

Be with us God and help us win this contest of today,
But let us hear with humble hearts the praises people say.

Let us be perfect in any form, and let each aim be true;
And let us take a certain pride in everything we do.

But fill our souls with honesty, and listen to our prayer,
That every time we play the game, we play it fair and square.

And every victory that we gain belongs at last to You,
Because You gave us all the strength to see each struggle through.

Amen

INTRODUCTION

It's been a long time – about thirty years I imagine – since I put pen to paper for a book. I told a little about my coaching philosophy and a lot about actual technique, a written basketball clinic as it were. My friend Paul Madison, Sports Information Director at Western Washington University, helped me with *Coach – God loves You – and so do I*. My thanks to Paul for his help on research for this book and for letting me recount some of the early events mentioned in my last book.

So much has happened since then –- both in my personal and professional life – that friends have encouraged me to tell the rest of the story. One of these, Rose Brittain, herself an entrepreneur, was particularly fascinated with my invention of the Slam-Dunk Rim, how it came to be, and how the legal system and perhaps my own trusting nature seemed to ace me out of a great deal of revenue. So that story is here, along with some wonderful memories of family, lifelong friends, and a basketball career I wouldn't trade for anything in the world. The honors and accolades I've received through the years are not due to my efforts alone. When one's name is engraved on a plaque or trophy or painted on a banner, it's because there's no room to write everyone's name who deserves to be on it. I share them all with my players, my assistant coaches, my loving wife, Doris, and even my mother, whose strict discipline and Christian values I passed along to my teams. Most of all, I share them with God, because without his guidance and love, nothing in my wonderful life would have happened and none of my "impossible" dreams would have come true.

Chuck Randall

PART ONE

LESSONS LEARNED

My life story isn't all that extraordinary – but the team of characters who have played a role in it, no matter how big or small, I feel *is* extraordinary. Some, such as John Wooden and Red Auerbach, are legendary in the world of sports; others, like my terrific granddaughter, Novella, have brought a special joy to my life.

But, I should start at the beginning, which was December 15, 1926, in Farmington, Washington. Dad was pretty well-known at the time as superintendent of schools. There was a newspaper article announcing my birth: "Mother and son are doing well, but it's not certain father will survive."

I grew up in nearby Veradale, just east of Spokane. Growing up in rural Washington, I was surrounded by women. Although my mother had died when I was in the fourth grade, there were still my three sisters and a cousin,

Novella Person Randall, Chuck's mom.

Lucy, who lived with us. I was the youngest so I guess I was pretty spoiled by the girls but not by my dad.

I can think of at least one instance when they literally, in fact permanently, saved my hide. My dad used to take a belt to me when he thought I deserved it. I would cry and cry. On one occasion, my pet dog, Punch, was in the room when Dad removed his belt to let me have it. Well, Punch put out the best growl he could muster, probably thinking it would save me, but Dad just removed him from the room and shut the door.

But this one time – I was ten years old – my sisters were there when Dad spanked me. I didn't shed a tear, but all three of them did. That was the last time Dad used a belt on me.

Arlie Jean was the oldest and really a source of pride for my father. She was really smart, a good student, and as a high school senior, valedictorian of her class. There was about eight years' difference between Jean and me.

Then came Ruth, two years younger than Jean. She became a very successful realtor. Her son Bob became a good high school basketball coach and was "Coach of the Year" four years in a row.

Joy was four years younger than Ruth and was my buddy. She was a real tomboy. Since she was just two years older than I, we walked to school together and played "Pump Pump Pull Away" in front of our house. That's where there were two goals, one at either end, and you'd try to run all of the way to the goal without getting tackled. Well, Joy could out-tackle some of the boys who were even older than she was.

She always liked hiking and biking, and at age eighty-one, she joined a group that was going to bike from northern Alaska to South America. Joy wanted to get up early, bike a few hours, stop a while to have lunch and rest, and then bike some more. Others in the group wanted to wait to start around 10 a.m., bike only a few hours, and then quit to camp the rest of the day. Joy decided that was not her cup of tea, so she stayed with them only four or five days.

Her next big goal was to be the oldest woman to climb Mount Rainier. She trained by doing cross-country skiing and bicycling, and at age eighty-two she did it in the summer of 2007! Because of the depth of the snow, she didn't reach the summit so that is still on her agenda.

I'm getting ahead of my story again!

Animals and sports were my two most favorite interests.

During summers, while I was in the third, fourth, and fifth grades, I would spend a week or two at my Uncle Wellie's farm in Curlew, a very beautiful, remote area in northern Washington, near the Canadian border. Now *that* was fun farming – getting to hike up the mountains, ride horses, and shoot a rifle.

Our farm, on the other hand, was sheer drudgery: weeding two and a half acres of land, milking two cows, feeding the pigs, and collecting eggs. I didn't like it at all. But then, academics sure weren't my thing either. I did only enough to graduate from high school so I could get into college, then only enough to graduate from college so I could enter a master's program, then only enough to get my master's in physical education from Washington State University. I figured I would need a master's degree in order to get a job on the college level.

I guess my spirit of competition developed even on the farm. I remember how we would put Punch, my Airedale, in the barn with my buddy Marv Ainsworth's pet collie, Pal. Marv and I would stand at an imaginary finish line about fifty yards away, then yell for my sister to open the barn door, and Punch and Pal would race to freedom while Marv and I would wildly cheer for our pet to see which one crossed the line first.

Up until fourth grade, I wanted to be a cowboy, but then something happened that summer that sparked a new interest I'd never felt before. I was visiting my Uncle Gene in Coeur d'Alene, Idaho. He was the high school football coach plus the track and field coach. He took me to a track meet in which his team was participating. I wasn't paying too much attention to the action until I noticed one of the athletes who had just completed a race went behind the grandstand and was crying. Now, to a fourth-grader, seeing a high school boy crying made a considerable impression. I ran to tell my uncle, who immediately went over to the kid. I saw him put his arm around him to comfort him, and I thought it was a wonderful gesture. The kid started smiling through his tears. I never forgot it, and I thought it must be just as important for a coach to show compassion toward his athletes as it is to show a team how to win.

From that time on, I wanted to be a coach.

Since baseball was my favorite sport then, I formed a neighborhood team with my best friend, Marv Ainsworth. The following year, we organized our own league consisting of four teams. Our team was the Vera Hotshots. I kept going back and forth between Simchuck's and another sporting goods store, trying to get a good deal on caps and shirts. I had both stores convinced that the other one was going to give us a better deal. We ended up with T-shirts with our team's name done by Simchuck's and got them for practically nothing. They even threw in a couple of bats! I made up a league schedule and reported the scores to the *Spokane Valley Herald*. We played a game at the All-Valley picnic that year and another under the lights. Wow! My first taste of crowds and glory. I liked it!

Then, in sixth grade, basketball took over my heart. My dad put up a hoop on our barn door, and I spent afternoons after school shooting baskets and working on my footwork.

My first year at Central Valley High School (1941), I made the freshman basketball team, which was coached by Ray Thacker. Later that winter, the varsity coach, Bill Lipscomb, took a carload of players, all seniors except me, to the state tournament. It was held at Hec Edmundson Pavilion on the University of Washington campus in Seattle. I had never seen such a huge gym in my life. The players looked like ants to me from my seat. I knew that I wanted to play there before my career was over.

I was in awe of the senior athletes, guys like Len Pyne, who was a neighbor. I tried to copy everything he did. One move I picked up from him (which I think he picked up from watching the Harlem Globetrotters) was where he would put the ball between his legs and fake like he was passing. When the defender looked where he thought the ball was going, Len would turn the other way and shoot.

Sig Hansen was the principal at Central Valley High, as well as my football coach. A very sentimental person, Sig showed me the heart and spirit aspects of coaching.

I remember that he often had the entire student body, myself included, in tears after he spoke at a pep assembly. While I was in high school, the Veradale Grade School basketball coach was drafted into the service, and I was asked to take over the team for him. So I conducted practice every day after my own was over. My team won the county title that year.

Coach Thacker was a real competitor and this rubbed off on me. I learned a lot about basketball from him. During my junior and senior years, our team won the county and district championships to earn trips to the state tournament. Because of my passing ability, I played at a high post position, in spite of the fact I was only 5′ 8″.

One of my closest friends in high school was Sandy Sinclair. He was a discus thrower and one spring he was consistently throwing beyond the existing state record. Everyone expected him to be the state champion. Although he broke the record at the state meet, another athlete tossed the discus even farther. This showed me that you must prepare not only to be good enough today, but also to be better for tomorrow. I ended high school lettering three years each in football, basketball, and baseball – but basketball definitely was where I saw my future.

Like most kids of the day, I was influenced greatly by my parents – their teaching, their discipline, their beliefs. Although my mother, who was a member of the Loyal Temperance Legion, died when I was in the fourth grade, her strong beliefs have stayed with me all my life. No smoking, no drinking in our household. My dad got his law degree at Willamette University in Salem, Oregon. As part of his law curriculum, he had to take U.S. history, which he really

Photo submitted by Harvey Shaw

Bears intent

Ray Thacker, with ball, had just taken over as head basketball coach for Central Valley High School in this photo from the early 1940s. Pictured in the back row, from left, were Chuck Randall, Bob Smith, Quenton Clark, Bud Waybright, Dick Campbell, Jim Morrow, Willy Dahl, Les Witt and Harvey Shaw; front row, Ed Stephens, coach Thacker and Dean Barth.

If you have an original historical photo you would like to see published, mail it to Historical Photos, 999 W. Riverside Ave., Spokane, WA 99201. Include a self-addressed, stamped envelope for return of your photo. We pay $20 for images we publish. Copies of most photos may be purchased by calling (509) 459-5416.

Ray Thacker, with the ball, had just become head basketball coach for Central Valley High School when this photo was taken in the early 1940s. Sophomore Chuck Randall is at far left.

liked, so he decided to pursue a teaching career. He got a job in the local high school but before long was named superintendent of schools. He didn't like that very much, so he left to go teach U.S. history in another school. Again, he was selected superintendent of schools. For the third time, he left, this time to teach history at North Central High School, where he stayed for twenty-five years. My dad implanted in me a love and devotion for my country. Being very religious people, both parents were persistent about my going to church every Sunday. It is a practice I have continued.

After graduating from high school, I went into the Army where I was trained as a paratrooper. I spent most of my time overseas in Japan during the occupation. As soon as I returned to Spokane, I began playing basketball again. I was planning to attend Whitworth College, but Red Reese, the coach at Eastern Washington University, encouraged me to enroll there instead. I played on the junior varsity team my first year.

The next season I met Ernie McKie, a transfer student. He and I became lifelong friends as well as business partners later on. Both of us happened to be cut from the basketball team that year, so we formed our own Amateur Athletic Union affiliated squad and beat such college teams as Whitworth and Gonzaga University. That experience made me especially selective when it came to finding players for my teams.

While at Eastern, one of the most important things in my life happened: I fell in love with a fellow student named Doris Reihl. I thought she was the prettiest girl on campus. We were married in August of 1948. As any coach will tell you, it takes a special kind of woman to be the wife of a coach. Her patience, understanding, and unconditional love have never wavered – well, hardly ever! – in nearly sixty years of marriage.

About seven years later (1955), while I was coaching at Lindbergh High School, my wife and I were at a church gathering with several other married couples when I mentioned to the Reverend Frank Sturdivant that I didn't know whether or not I was really helping the world through coaching. My grandmother had always wanted one of her grandchildren to become a missionary. Perhaps that was my calling.

The minister said, "Chuck, I think you could do more good for the world by bringing your Christian beliefs into your coaching." And so this is what I did – and as a result, coaching came to have more meaning and purpose to me.

Senior photo.

MY WAR STORY

World War II was well under way while I was in high school. I turned eighteen in December during my senior year, so I was drafted. Since I was on the basketball team and Ray Thacker, my coach, must have thought he needed me, I got deferred until June of that year (1945).

I was shipped to Camp Roberts, twelve miles north of Paso Robles, about halfway between San Francisco and Los Angeles, for seventeen weeks of basic training. Basic training, of course, was designed to be very strenuous to see if we could handle tough situations. Though I'd never done it before in my life, I pretty near started drinking coffee for the first time on some bivouacs – they were mighty cold early mornings!

We also had to keep our rifles spotless. Well, of course, shooting shells over and over dirtied our rifles, and some of the guys didn't want that to happen so they gave me all the shells they didn't shoot. I didn't hesitate and shot over a hundred times, not realizing at the time that I was damaging my hearing. I'm sure that is why today I have hearing loss.

At the end of seventeen weeks, I had the option of where to go for specialized training. The army paratrooper school was in Fort Benning, Georgia. I felt I would gain more respect from family and friends at home if I became a paratrooper instead of a regular GI – even though I was afraid of heights! I had to do six jumps – five in basic training.

By the time I finished that four-week training, I was thankful the war had ended because paratroopers had been shipped regularly overseas and dropped into action. Money was somewhat of a motivation, too – a PFC paratrooper made as much as a lieutenant in regular service. But you had to jump to get jump pay, so I jumped again in Japan.

Because the war was ending, before we were shipped out, we were allowed to go home for one week at Christmastime. So from Fort Benning I went home to Veradale so I could see all of my friends and family before heading overseas. That was one of the few times I realized that my dad really did care about me because there were tears in his eyes as he said goodbye. From Veradale, I took a Greyhound bus to Fort Lawton in Seattle where we boarded the boat for Yokohama.

There were so many soldiers on the ship to Japan that we were stacked four- and five-deep in bunks. And,

He's in the Army now.

mealtimes were a real hassle. The lines were so long that when we finished breakfast, we'd get in line for lunch, and as soon as we finished lunch, we'd get in line for dinner! I got tired of that real fast so I offered my services as a flunky. Smart move – I got the job! From then on, I had a meal pass so I didn't have to stand in line but could go right into the galley. I didn't have any work to speak of, and I got to eat really well.

My division, the 11th Airborne, was stationed in Sendai, in northern Japan, so after spending a day or so in Yokohama, we were put on a train for the day-long trip to Sendai.

My first day there, I was given the job of watching over Japanese people digging a ditch. As I stood watching them, I could hear what I thought was a basketball bouncing in a large building nearby, and naturally, having basketball fever, I couldn't pass up checking it out. When I got there, I discovered that at one end of the gym they were having baseball tryouts, and the coach, Major Fitzgibbons – everybody called him Fitz – asked, "Are you here to try out for the baseball team?"

I said, "If I could, I'd sure like to."

At noon that day, they produced a cut list – players who did not make the team – and my name was on it. Players that got cut had the day off so they all went into town, but I had to stay to watch the people digging the ditch.

I left the ditch diggers again and went back into the gym to watch the afternoon tryouts. Coach Fitz was catching batting practice. He was down on one knee with his right hand behind his back to keep from getting injured. After a while, he asked if someone would relieve him, and I volunteered. I got down on one knee and did exactly as I had seen him do. Some of the players really got a kick out of seeing this and started calling me "Fitz Junior."

Coach Fitz asked if I'd join the team as batting practice catcher. I was tickled to have the chance and went back to the barracks to inform our first sergeant that I was going to be with the baseball team. He was quite angry that I was getting involved with baseball instead of watching his ditch diggers. He sent me to the barracks and said, "You wait there!"

I went to the gym and told Coach Fitz what the sergeant had said. Fitz said, "You go get all your things and come right back to the gym." So I did. Well, of course, this didn't sit too well with the sergeant. I'd see guys from our platoon at the baseball games and they'd say, "You don't want to ever come back."

Our commander, General Joe "Jumping Joe" Swing, it turned out, was a real baseball fan. After I was done with batting practice, he wanted me to sit in the stands with him during the game to identify who the different players were. The players were either ex-pro ballplayers or former college players, not high school athletes like I was. When my buddies saw me with the general, they figured I would have no further trouble with the sergeant!

Players were being shipped home so I got to be a second-string catcher and eventually a starter. We played in great stadiums all over, including Tokyo and Yokohama. This was great baseball country; there were sometimes as many as thirty to forty thousand people at a game.

At Koshien Stadium, near Osaka, the oldest and most famous ballpark in Japan, I was surprised to see a statue of Babe Ruth. Ruth had played there in exhibition games in 1934. I have a lasting memory of that stadium because in one game, Lefty Verderain was pitching and I was catching. I heard Lefty had been a pitcher in the Pacific Coast League prior to the service. He struck out eighteen batters at Koshien, a record for the stadium. And, of course, because I was part of the battery, my name appears alongside his in the record books.

As players from our baseball team got shipped home, everyone wanted to drink a farewell toast to them. Even though I was now drinking age and they insisted I join them, I never forgot my mother's teachings and was against it. When they weren't looking, I'd dump my drink into the flower pot!

I got acquainted with a lot of great players and athletes during that time. Only two of them on the team were seen or heard of after we left Japan: Bill Sampson, who ended up pitching for the Spokane Indians of the Northwest League, and Jack Swarthout, who went on to become a highly successful football coach and athletic director at the University of Montana.

Many years later, I was attending an Old Timers Basketball Coaches banquet where Judd Heathcote was guest speaker. Judd coached at West Valley High School while I was at Lindbergh High. Later, he went to Washington State as assistant coach to Marv Harshman, then went to Montana as head coach, and finally ended his career at Michigan State, where his Spartans won the national championship in 1979.

At the banquet, he recalled his Montana days and spoke highly of Jack Swarthout, which brought back all of my old Army memories. Judd also praised Indiana's Bobby Knight, who had been a rival coach thirty-seven times during his career. I was happy to hear this as I always felt that Bobby Knight had a good relationship with his players or they wouldn't have put up with his toughness.

Back to my war story…

At the end of the baseball season, it looked like I had to go back to my platoon and my loving sergeant. I wasn't looking forward to that. But then, as luck would have it, they gave the baseball players a chance to turn out for the division football team. That sounded good to me, so I turned out for the football team to prolong my return to the platoon.

I turned out for quarterback. They were keeping three only, and wouldn't you know it, I was the fourth! I thought I was doomed but then the coach asked if I wanted to stay on as a manager. "Sure," I said. I stayed with the football team until I was to ship back to the States.

Another memorable moment was when I got to meet General Douglas MacArthur after a game in Tokyo. He addressed the team and said, "If any of you want to go to West Point, I can help you get in." I was just a manager so I figured he wasn't talking to me!

As they were processing us to go home, they went through all of our gear. They took out any items from Japan. I had collected a lot of great things, which I couldn't bring home. The ship filled up just before they got to my name. It looked as though I, maybe, would have to wait a few more days – or even weeks. I had been there almost a year by now. I was anxious to get home.

A few of the fellows chided me, "Since you're such a buddy of Joe Swing, why don't you get him to get you on the boat!"

Of course, I didn't, and to pass the time, a bunch of us went to a movie, which we weren't supposed to do. When I returned, there was a Report to Headquarters note waiting. This time I thought I was really in trouble. Instead, I found out I would be in the next group to fly home. I toyed with the idea of meeting the ship when it came in and telling everyone, "Joe Swing set me up." But I didn't.

I went home to Spokane Valley in hopes of enrolling in some college. I turned out with the Whitworth College basketball team and then got a phone call from Red Reese, coach at Eastern Washington University, asking me to come talk to him. He said I could play on the JV team the rest of the year and not lose a year of my eligibility. I agreed to go to Eastern, a life-changing event for me because that's where I met that prettiest girl on campus. We met at a dance, just about one of the last dances I've ever been to. I asked her out and found out she was also one of the smartest girls on campus.

That spring of 1947, I played on the baseball team as second-string catcher, which meant that I didn't catch unless there was a doubleheader. But by the time the season was over, I was catching full time.

I remember we played a championship game on the University of Washington baseball field. Although I had a weak arm, I caught the first guy trying to steal. Luckily, they didn't try to steal again. I had a good day at bat and made what everyone thought was a spectacular catch when my cleats slipped on the concrete on the front side of the backstop and I caught a pop foul while I was falling. I'm sure I would never have caught that ball if I hadn't fallen.

The prettiest, and the smartest, girl on campus – Doris Reihl.

Nevertheless, I was named Most Valuable Player of the game, and we became league champions.

The following year, when I got cut from the baseball team, people said, "How could they cut the MVP?" *I* knew why. I didn't have a good arm, and I was a slow runner. Since I wasn't playing in any sport, my intention was to get out of school ASAP so I could get out and coach. I went to summer school and took all the credits I could cram in every chance I got.

The next year, I got cut from the basketball team too, along with my friend, Ernie McKie. So we started our own AAU team, sponsored by Brownson Motors. We played in the city league and were quite competitive. Judd Heathcote played in that same league so we got re-acquainted. In extra games, we played Whitworth College and Gonzaga University. Eastern's JV at that time was as good or better than the Varsity. We beat all of them. Reese went to McKie after we played the Varsity and asked him to come back on his team, but Ernie turned him down.

Playing basketball with Ernie was the start of a lifetime friendship. McKie and I and our wives vacationed together in Noxon, Montana, where Ernie grew up. We were supposed to be able to catch landlocked salmon there, each big enough to fill a quart jar. As it turned out, it would take four of what *we* caught to fill a quart jar, plus we had a hard time catching them anyway. We also took several twelve-mile hiking trips through the mountains to Wanless Lake. Those trips cemented our friendship as well as our love of basketball.

Chuck and Doris are wed, August 22, 1948.

Doris and I were married in August of 1948. To earn money while going to summer school, I drove the school bus to Liberty Lake for recreation outings with a bunch of kids. I was also the lifeguard. These were long, long days – starting early in the morning, with a full load of classes at Eastern, then picking up the kids for swimming, and then taking them back to the high school for the young kids' baseball program, and then driving back to Eastern and home to our trailer court. I think with this job and the GI Bill, we were able to do okay financially. We could even afford to pay when we went to the movies instead of sneaking in!

One day, after one of these fifteen- to sixteen-hour days, I was supposed to pick up Doris in Spokane and bring her home. I totally forgot and went straight home. When she wasn't there, I figured she must be visiting her friend, Molly Clark. I went to bed, and the next morning she still wasn't there. I found out that when I didn't show up, she had called my sister for a ride and spent the night at her home. She caught a bus to Eastern the next morning. Needless to say, she wasn't very happy with me. And come to think of it, how does one misplace his wife? Luckily she forgave me, and we're still married.

During spring quarter, Ernie was asked to play in a basketball tournament back East. He got excuses from all of his classes. At the end of the quarter, when our grades came out, he got a B instead of an A in physiology. Not known to be particularly shy, he wrote a letter to the president of the college and said he had been excused from that class and thought the only reason he got the B was because he had gone to this tournament. He offered to take a test and even challenged the teacher to take the same test. It was to no avail. But Ernie and the teacher were not done with each other. During summer quarter, we were both taking anatomy from the same teacher. She tried to stump Ernie, but he always knew the correct answers. From then on, when she made a point, she always asked, "Is that right, Mr. McKie?" He had won her over!

MORE LESSONS LEARNED

It was a real struggle to get ahead in the beginning of my coaching career. After four years at Opportunity Grade School in Washington, from 1949 to 1953, my team had compiled a record of 54-6. I didn't feel much challenged, but boy, I had no idea what challenges lay ahead for me!

I got the break I'd been looking for by getting a position at Riverside High School. The students there, by and large, were good, solid farm kids, but there were also a number of kids who had been expelled from nearby John Rogers High School. After a school dance, all of the players on my team, except for one senior and one junior, broke my training rules: no smoking or drinking. I had to kick them all off the team except those two, which left me with just two upper-classmen. The squad was mostly sophomores, but even so, we ended that '53-'54 season with a 12-8 record, better than the school's three previous seasons combined.

That summer, Alex Ripple, the superintendent of Republic School District, called to ask if I would coach at his high school. He knew about my philosophy concerning training. Since I had a bunch of good young kids coming back at Riverside, I didn't want to leave. So, I declined his offer.

The next day, he came to our home and asked me what it would take to get me to come to Republic. Since I didn't really want the job, I made some pretty big requests, especially considering the fact that I had coached just one year at the high school level. I asked for five hundred dollars more than I was currently earning, a teaching job for my wife, an assistant coach of my choosing, and a home.

Much to my surprise, he agreed to all of my terms. I still didn't really want to go, so I told him I would have to take a look at the school and town before making a decision. We couldn't find a home we liked, and I discovered that the gymnasium was in pretty bad shape.

"We'll build a house for you," said Ripple. "And," he added, "we'll remodel the gym." He was even going to have a house built right next door to us for my assistant, Sandy Sinclair.

I was still hedging about accepting the job when we stopped by a lake located near the town. He opened the trunk of his car and took out a fishing rod. "Like to fish?" he asked.

I'd loved fishing since I was a kid so he didn't have to ask twice. "Sure do," I said.

Chuck (3) was a member of the 1950-51 champion team in the
Boots & Saddle Club.
L/R Sandy Sinclair, Del Muse, Carl Dahl, Quentin Clark,
Al Strohmeir, Chuck Randall, Ernie McKie,
Andy Anderson (manager).

"Here, use my pole." And, on my first cast, I caught a three-pound rainbow. "I'll take the job," I told him. That meant coaching football and baseball as well as basketball, but I didn't care – I was caught, hook, line, and sinker!

It quickly became apparent to me that Republic was a pretty tough town. I began to worry about how the athletes would accept my training rules. Right away, I learned from one of my athletes, Skip Laurie, that the previous year the coach and players had smoked together in the locker room at halftime! I knew I had my work cut out for me.

Soon after football practice began, I was forced to dismiss an athlete from the team for not training. Though it was just as difficult for me as it was for him, it turned out to be a blessing in disguise because it showed the other players that I meant business. I had no further problems the rest of the season. What's more, we finished with a 4-2-1 record, a big improvement over the previous year, and we nearly took the league championship.

This spirit carried through to the basketball season.

One of the players on the basketball squad was Jerry Martin, whose large family lived in a one-room house fifteen miles from school. Jerry's dad was a logger who spent a lot of his free time in the local tavern.

During football season, Jerry had hitchhiked home after turnout, but basketball presented a problem. A mountain pass between his home and school was often closed, so it looked as though he wouldn't be able to participate.

As a rule, I didn't have players stay at my house, but I figured this was a special situation. I had Jerry come and live with us for the winter. He was a great kid, and we became good friends. Although not a talented ballplayer, he was very serious about the game and put everything he had into it.

Toward the end of the season, there was a big school dance. Jerry was really excited about going. Since he didn't have a suit of his own, he borrowed mine.

At around ten o'clock the night of the dance, Doris and I decided to go over to see how things were going. That was pretty easy as our house was located near the gym where the dance was being held. As we walked in, we noticed Jerry sitting in a corner by himself. He was usually a very outgoing, friendly guy so we knew this wasn't like him at all.

I went over to him and asked if anything was wrong. He looked up and asked me to follow him.

We went down to the locker room where Jerry told me that before going to the dance, he had gone over to the tavern to get some money from his father. "My dad told me he wouldn't let me have the money unless I had a drink of beer," he said. "So, I took a sip, grabbed the money, and left. Afterwards, I felt really bad because I had let you and the whole team down by not keeping training."

I knew that Jerry figured I would dismiss him from the team. Instead, I told him that he had already punished himself enough, and as far as I was concerned, that was the end of it.

I tell this story to illustrate the importance of a coach having a love for, as well as a discipline of, his players. There is a fine line between the two and a coach must know how to give and take in every situation that comes along.

GOD'S GAME PLAN

We weren't real successful at Republic, but the attitude of the players never wavered. In fact, the sports reporter for the Wenatchee newspaper wrote that our team was the most improved and that the players had the best attitude of any team in the entire league.

I only stayed one year. I was looking forward to getting back to Spokane Valley. My friend Del Muse's dad was superintendent of schools in Valleyford, Washington. He approached me to see if I'd take the basketball and baseball coaching job at Lindbergh High School, to start in the 1955-56 season. Since my buddy Sandy Sinclair would be my replacement at Republic, I knew they would be in good hands.

I have many fond memories of my years at Lindbergh High. Shortly after I was hired, I attended the school's spring picnic. There, I met all of the team candidates, which wasn't too difficult in a school with only seventy students. I told the aspirants that our goal was to win the state championship. In order to do that, we had to pay a price not only during the season, but through the off-season as well. There were no summer camps at that time, so I told them I'd open up the gym on Tuesday and Thursday nights for practice.

Their eyes really lit up at this proposal, but when I suggested seven o'clock as the starting time, they quickly dimmed. Finally, one boy gingerly raised his hand and asked if the time could be moved ahead to nine o'clock. We put it to a vote and every player was in favor of nine o'clock, so that was set as the start of practice time.

The first night of turnout, I arrived at the gym around eight thirty, and no one was there. At eight forty-five, still no one had shown up. Then, at five minutes to nine, a number of cars pulled up and in came the kids. I couldn't believe what I saw: Everyone was black from head to toe. They had the dirtiest faces you could imagine. I learned that they had been hauling hay since six that morning and then had come directly to the gym. Some hadn't even eaten dinner. I still remember seeing the sweat leave clean streaks as it ran down their faces during practice.

Well, this went on twice a week all summer-long. Talk about falling in love with kids – a pretty easy thing to do with a bunch of guys who would work in the hayfields all day and then show up to play basketball on their own for two hours.

We were picked to finish near the bottom of the league in pre-season polls. Our main weakness was lack of height.

At Lindbergh High, Chuck taught U.S. History, Washington State History, and Athletics. Back row: Randall, Mr. Fuller, Mr. Cameron; front row: Mrs. Smith, Mrs. Muse, Mrs. Garner.

The starting five consisted of 5'8"twin brothers, Larry and Gary Owens, at guards; 5'11" Dan Jeremiah and 6'1" Gary Bonzer, forwards; and 6'2" Roy Emtman at center.

The sixth man was Jack Blaine. He had played as a freshman, but polio had kept him from participating the next two years. Although his movement was hampered, he was a fine shooter.

The season began and we won game after game. The guys did everything I asked of them. I've never had a ball club put forth more effort as consistently as this one did. Training was no problem to this team; that was their life-style year-round. They didn't even swear.

We ended the regular season with a 17-6 record, which earned us a berth in the county tournament. There, in the first game, we defeated Riverside 43-33, which put us in the championship game the next night against Medical Lake.

Medical Lake had a formidable team with no starter under 6' 2". At halftime, we were down by 25 points. They were just too big and strong for us to handle. During half-time intermission, I couldn't think of much to say since the team was giving its all. But I did tell them that we had too much invested in the season not to go out and do every-thing we could to win.

The second half was a fantastic thing to watch. I've never seen a ball club play like Lindbergh High did that half. They dove for loose balls and hustled every second, despite the fact that they couldn't cut into that deficit. I've never witnessed such sustained effort, with no hint of giv-ing up, by a team so outmanned, before or since.

The loss paired us against Riverside the next night in the consolation game, which would determine the second berth to the district tournament.

It was a close game throughout, but the effort of the night before had really taken its toll. Still, with twenty seconds remaining, we trailed by only two points, 52-50. Riverside had the ball and was stalling. With five seconds left, Larry Owens stole the ball. Because time was nearly up, he had to stop and shoot the ball from twenty feet out. As the shot was midway to the basket, the buzzer sounded. The ball went into the basket, spun around and around for what seemed an eternity, and then popped out. The season was over.

On the way home, I had the first six players in my car. Nobody said a word the whole way. Finally we got back to school. It was then that Larry asked me, "Coach, how can a guy pray to a God who would let that ball go out instead of in?"

It's a pretty serious time in a person's life when he asks such a question, and it's a tough one to answer. All I could say at the time was, "Larry, I don't know right now. I kind of feel like you do. It's hard to believe that God would let such a thing happen."

Instead of going into the school and putting the gear away, we just stayed in the car and talked. The conversation touched upon such topics as school, girls, life goals. We also discussed what great team relations we had and how the members of the team hoped they would always remain lifelong friends.

We were still talking at four in the morning. Later, I learned from my wife that every player's mother had phoned, wondering where her boy was. Doris assured them that they were not to worry; they were in good hands with their coach. Even if we'd had cell phones in those days, I'm not so sure we would have thought to call home. We were in an unforgettable moment of true friendship.

Finally, we took the gear into school, and I began taking the players home. The first house we came to was that of Larry and Gary Owens.

As he got out of the car, Larry stopped and said, "Coach, I figured out how come God let that ball go out. If we had won that game, we would have been happy about going to the District, but the fact that we lost and had this time together tonight has tied us even closer together. Having this team relationship is better than going to District or State. God has really brought us close, and I feel we'll be close friends the rest of our lives."

That was more than fifty years ago. Long after that season, when my Western team was playing in Spokane, I went out to Valleyford to visit Larry. While I was there, nearly every member of that team stopped by at some time during the day. They hadn't been told I was there. They have just continued to be the closest of friends.

It is players such as these and events such as these that make coaching so rewarding. Winning, I feel, is secondary to both, though striving to win helped make each a reality.

I believe Larry was right – God had his own Game Plan that night, and we were all the better for it.

SOMETHING EXTRA

Two years after I went to Lindbergh High, Lindbergh was consolidated with Rockford, becoming Freeman High, and we continued to have winning seasons.

A few years later, in 1958, I was hired as the coach at Lind High School in a small town about fifteen miles south of Ritzville. There were only about sixty kids in the whole school. Although we were successful there too, in looking back I realize it was a big mistake to leave Freeman. It was the only time in my career that I let money influence my decision. They offered me several thousand dollars more a year. I stayed at Lind for three years, but I think I probably would have been even more successful at Freeman.

Well, during all of the years I was coaching in high school, I had a personal goal someday to become a coach at a college or university. Even with my winning records, I wasn't making much headway toward that objective. In order to have a chance at moving up, I had to do something extra.

In the spring of 1959, I applied for the coaching job at Bellingham High School, thinking that if I could do well there, I might have a chance to land a job at Western Washington University located in the same city. But, I was runner-up for the post. That seemed to happen frequently.

A turning point in my life occurred that summer when I drove to a basketball clinic at Glacier National Park in northwestern Montana. The featured speaker was one of the greatest college coaches of that time, Adolph Rupp, from the University of Kentucky. As part of his talk, Rupp mentioned a camp on the East Coast where the sport was taught to boys during the summer months.

While driving back home, I began thinking that if Rupp had not been able to be there, I could have given the clinic for him. Of course I had less experience, but I had read many books on basketball and had attended numerous clinics – enough so that I considered myself a pretty good student of the game. Then I got to thinking about the camp Rupp had talked about. If I could start one in our area, it might help me land a college coaching position.

My original plan was to involve a "name" coach like Marv Harshman, who was then at Washington State University, and other high school coaches. We would go to each school in and around the Spokane area, presenting clinics. Players selected from each of the schools could participate in an All-Star game. Admission could be charged to this contest, which would reduce the amount each boy would have to pay to attend the sessions.

By the time I got home from Montana, I was really excited about the idea and eager to tell my wife. When I arrived home, two friends happened to be visiting – Otto Lobe, chairman of the school board, and his wife, Sarah. I shared my idea with them and when Otto learned that I wanted to take a trip east to see a camp first-hand, he told me I should do it. That's all the encouragement I needed; within the next two hours, I was on a Greyhound bus headed for New York City.

We had a brief layover in Boise, Idaho, so I called my former high school P.E. teacher, Bill Everts, who was now the city's recreation director. We met and talked about my idea, and the more we talked the more I became convinced that it would be better to have only one campsite, open to anyone who wanted to attend.

I arrived in New York early Saturday morning. I looked in the phone book for the National Basketball Association because I thought that would be a good place to start. Its address was in the Empire State Building so I headed there. Much to my dismay, it was closed on Saturdays, so I stopped in a large sporting goods store and asked the owner where I could locate a basketball camp. He said the only one he knew of was at Kutsher's Resort in the Catskill Mountains. I didn't ask any more questions. I boarded a bus for the four-hour trip to the resort.

When I got there, I found that the resort catered to very wealthy people, and basketball was played there by outstanding college players from all over the country, who performed for the guests at night. They were directed by Red Auerbach, coach of the Boston Celtics, at that time the top professional team in America.

I went to the office of the resort's owner, Milt Kutsher. His secretary said he was busy and asked me to leave my name and number where I was staying. I told her if she didn't mind I'd just wait there until he could see me. Since they knew I wasn't going anywhere, a few minutes later Kutsher came out of his office. I found he loved basketball as much as I did, and when he found out what I did back home, he put me up free of charge for two days. He introduced me to Red Auerbach and even offered to set me up with my own camp in New York. But I wasn't interested in staying on the East Coast.

The next two days were really enjoyable as I got to know Auerbach. He seemed to enjoy talking to me too, since I was the only "basketball coach type" around who could share experiences and talk the same language. He told me that the type of camp I was looking for was located along the Hudson River. It was run by Clair Bee, another outstanding coach at City College of New York. Auerbach introduced me to an attorney whose son attended that camp and also wrote a letter of introduction for me to Clair Bee. The attorney gave me a ride to the camp, and Bee turned out to be very generous with his time and ideas about how to set up a similar camp in the Northwest.

Soon after I returned to Spokane, I attended another clinic at Whitworth College. There, I ran into my high school coach, Ray Thacker, and my best friend, Ernie McKie, who also was coaching in that area. When I told them of my plan, they shared my enthusiasm, and we decided to become partners in the venture.

Every weekend that fall, I looked for a campsite. We eventually decided upon Conifer Lodge on Snoqualmie

Pass. That winter, we mailed out brochures and applications to every high school coach in Oregon, Idaho, Montana, Washington, and British Columbia. Nearly 450 boys, aged twelve to eighteen, signed up.

In March, I went to the Pass to look at the lodge and to see how work was going on the courts and swimming pool. Because of the snow, nothing had been started, but I was assured by the owner that everything would be ready by the middle of June when the camp was scheduled to begin. In May, I returned and still nothing had been done. Finally, I took our attorney up for a look. He said there was no way the camp would be finished in time and that it would probably be useless to file suit.

Well, McKie was up in Alaska fishing, so Thacker and I moved into the lodge and began working to get the camp ready. For three weeks, we worked an average of fourteen hours a day, supervising the bigger jobs, and we completed the task in time.

Word spread about the camp, and I was excited at this new opportunity to hone the skills of young boys interested in basketball. They came from everywhere for the week-long sessions – except Montana, which at that time did not allow youngsters to participate.

In New York, they charged each boy $100 a week for camp. We ran Sunday night to Saturday afternoon, provided three meals a day, plus bedding. We held a big awards banquet on Saturday night, got the best coaches in the Pacific Northwest – including Marv Harshman, Paul Velanti, and Dean Nicholson – and charged $69.50 for the week. We had 120 at a time, and the opening season enrolled 500 boys. Eventually, we had close to 1,000.

Conifer, the first such camp west of New York, was another 'impossible dream' come true for founder Chuck Randall. Participating instructors included Red Reese, Marv Harshman, Steve Belko, John Grayson, Joe Cipriano, Mac Duckworth, Al Negratti, and Don Barnette, along with owners Randall, Ray Thacker, and Ernie McKie.

Conifer Athletic Camp at Snoqualmie Pass (1970).

While the camp was in progress, several athletic types from California paid us a visit.

"You should start a camp like this in California," they urged. That seemed like a pretty good idea.

◁ ◁ ◁

A year later, in 1961, my partners and I decided to set up another camp, this time in California. My sister Ruth lived in Culver City, so I stayed with her while I scouted out places to hold the camp. I was driving up in the San Bernardino Mountains looking for a ski resort. Snow Valley had the most to offer. They had a ski lift that one could take to go hiking, a great lodge, and a fine restaurant that attracted lots of people.

I talked to the owner about putting in a basketball court for a summer camp. When he heard how successful the Conifer camp was, he agreed. I recruited quite a stellar list of coaches, including John Wooden, Bill Sharman, and supposedly Elgin Baylor, spectacular player for the Lakers. I say "supposedly" because even though I had written to invite him to participate, I never got a reply. Then, one day, I heard him being interviewed and he was asked if he had any plans for the summer, and he said, "Oh, yeah, I'm going to be coaching at a basketball camp in Snow Valley." That was news to me – but good news – so I added him to our brochure. When the time came for his clinic, however, we never saw him. So I called the Lakers, and he wasn't there. Hot Rod Hundley was there at the time, and he agreed to take Elgin Baylor's place. This turned out well because he did a great job.

We did a lot of promotion for the camp. We sent out thousands of brochures. One day as I was driving around, I saw a sign outside a radio station: "THE LARGEST RADIO LISTENING AUDIENCE IN THE WORLD." I thought to myself: "That would be good exposure." So I went inside and told them about the camp.

I said, "We're trying to reach every boy we can as this is a first for California." The sports director thought it was a great idea. It was Mother's Day weekend so he recorded tapes of himself, John Wooden, and me announcing the camp. Every three hours, they were rotated, Friday night to Monday morning. Then, at one of the baseball games in L.A., I stood at home plate and made an announcement before the game.

We had so much hype about our camp that we were sure the Snow Valley camp would have a huge turnout. We expected over a thousand kids, but much to our surprise only about 250 enrolled that first year. From then on, it grew and grew, and I hear that the camp continues going even today.

The first summer there, I gave a clinic which was heard by Warren MacQueen, the superintendent of the El Segundo school district, who was on vacation there. Afterwards we talked and he asked me if I would be interested in the head coaching position that had just opened at his high school, which would be the largest I had ever coached at.

Two days later, I went to take a look at the school. The gym was fantastic. It had a seating capacity of 2,000, much bigger than any I had ever coached in before. The salary offer was also $4,000 more than I was getting at the time.

While there, I met Andy Anderson, a 6′3″ left-handed forward, who apparently was the best returning player, even though he had been the seventh man the year before. Andy told me that the previous year's team had placed second in their league and would have won the championship if the players had been disciplined and trained.

He said, "If you handle that part, I'll do the rest to make sure we win."

I was undecided. I didn't really want to leave Lind High School. Practically my whole team was returning, and I also had a game scheduled with Central Valley High, whose team was directed by my camp partner and former coach, Ray Thacker.

I went to see Ray, and he didn't hesitate. "Go," he said. "This will be a great opportunity for you."

So I accepted the job.

Within the first two months of my teaching P.E. at El Segundo High, a student got hit by a bat that had slipped out of a player's hand. I had to take him to the school nurse. Two weeks later, while climbing the rope in the gym, another kid fell and sprained his ankle. I took him to the nurse. Right after that, the principal called me into his office and said,

"There are some teachers we know we want to come back next year, some we're not sure about, and some we're sure we *don't* want – and you fall in the third group!"

Within the next week or two, while I was teaching P.E., everyone in the class urged me to wrestle John Brett, one of the school's best wrestlers and a very strong guy. I obliged. He immediately got me in a scissors hold, but I had learned from my cousin, JT, that you could break that hold by crossing your legs over the top of your opponent's and then straightening them out. I did this – and proceeded to break John's leg! Well, if I didn't think it before, at that point I thought maybe I shouldn't have bought a house in El Segundo! By the way, John is the older brother of baseball's George Brett. Hm-m, wonder if they remember this incident!

The basketball season began, and we lost five of our first eight games. Even worse than our record was the student body's attitude toward basketball. Despite the huge gym, only a small number of people came to our home games. The cheerleaders didn't even show up! They figured their job was over with the end of the football season. Needless to say, I was disappointed, but I still felt we had a fine team.

Before league play began, there was a break for the Christmas holidays. On New Year's Day, I went to the Rose Bowl game with the sports editor of our local newspaper. As we were heading home, I told him that if he wanted to be known as a great forecaster he should pick El Segundo to win the league championship. That would be quite a statement since all of the other polls had tabbed us to finish last. Well, the next day's paper predicted that we would win the title all right, but it had ME making the prediction!

In our first league contest, we lost in overtime to Aviation High School. Things looked pretty bleak, but due primarily to the drive of Anderson and players like Kirk Brown, Dan Deurwaarder, and Larry Sligar, we began winning.

In fact, we won all of the rest of our league games, except the last one, to win the Pioneer League title for the

*El Segundo High's Andy Anderson (left) and Larry Sligar with
new coach, Chuck Randall.*

first time since 1936 and qualify for the California Inter-scholastic Federation (CIF) playoffs.

Things really turned around with student support during this stretch of success, but there were also some discipline problems among the students. One was the "Phantom Crapper," who left his calling card in, among other places, the middle of the gym floor and on the principal's desk. Another was the shooting off of firecrackers in the school building. Things got so bad that the principal threatened to expel any student caught doing it.

Not long after this edict, we clinched the title with an overtime win at Torrance High School. After the game, while I was talking with the opposing coach, there was a terrific explosion in our locker room.

When I walked in, not one player said a word. Finally, Andy, who was the captain, said, "Coach, we were so happy over winning that I thought I'd light this firecracker. But as soon as I did, I knew I shouldn't have, so I threw it in the toilet."

I walked over to where the toilet should have been, but wasn't. Instead, there was porcelain everywhere. I told Andy he would have to pay for the repairs and miss the next game. Fortunately, and probably in part due to our success, the principal went along with my disciplinary measures and didn't insist on any additional punishment.

In the CIF playoffs, we defeated L.B. Millikan High School 47-46 with a basket in the final seconds. I remember being carried off the floor along with Deurwaarder, who had made the winning shot. It was the first-ever win for El Segundo in this, its third playoff appearance.

The next night we lost 48-40 to Chaffey High, and our season was over.

The following day, Andy came to see me and to apologize for not playing well in the loss. He said that his back was really bothering him. We went to a doctor and discovered that he had a slipped disc. For the life of me, I don't know how he was able to play ball at all, much less well enough that I didn't realize he was hurting. But this was the kind of person Andy was.

By springtime of that school year, the principal was prepared to fire the football coach. When I entered the school one day, there were a bunch of students sitting outside. I asked them what they were doing, and they said they refused to go in because the coach was going to be fired. The principal then called an assembly and told them he had decided not to fire him after all. But almost immediately, when the principal went before the school board, they overruled him and instructed him to fire the coach anyway. He knew the student body would raise havoc when he called another assembly to tell them the news. He asked me to wait behind the curtain in case there was trouble because he felt I was the only one who could calm them down. After making the announcement, the principal told everyone school was dismissed, so there was no trouble after all. I think the kids were just happy to get out of school early. But, by then he had realized, too, what a great relationship I had with my students. What's more, at the start of the season, when we had been picked to be at the bottom of our league, he never came to the games either. But after we continued winning, he started coming to games and parading back and forth across the floor. By winning the championship, we had gained new fans, in both the administration and the student body, and the cheerleaders even showed up.

My winning record that first year (18-8) had considerable impact on my career. A position at Western Washington State College opened the following summer and a friend, Joe Moses, went over to apply for it. When he found out the salary – only $6,000 a year – he knew he didn't want the job and instead told me I should apply. The pay was about half what I was making at El Segundo, and the principal even offered me a raise if I would stay, but my long-awaited dream was finally going to come true. I applied for the job at Western and got it.

Andy wanted to come and play for me, but he lived with his mother and didn't want to leave her alone. Instead, he attended El Camino Junior College for two years, then enrolled in the University of Southern California, keeping in touch with me through letters.

Soon after graduation from USC, Andy went into the service. He wrote to tell me he loved his country and wanted to serve her any way he could. Five months later, while I was at my camp on Snoqualmie Pass, I received a phone call from Kirk Brown, Andy's close friend. Andy had been killed in action in Vietnam. Kirk wanted to share a letter Andy had written shortly before his death. In it, he told how close he felt to me, that I was like a father to him.

That night, I walked out of the lodge and looked up at the clear night sky. The stars shone so brightly that it seemed as though Andy was right there with me. It was quite a feeling.

I'll always remember Andy. He came to mean a lot to me, even though I coached him for only that one year. He was a great competitor, always hustling and playing with all the energy he had in him. That's the way he played so I know that's how he fought. Bullets don't really stop guys like that; they just go through them.

As for the camps, Conifer went on for fourteen years. During that time, we changed sites twice, moving to Mount St. Michael's Seminary, then Holiday Hills, both located near Spokane. Although it was the first such camp west of New York, by the time it closed there were literally hundreds of similar camps in operation.

The camp was good to me – both professionally and financially. But better still, through it I had the opportunity to meet a lot of great people who have remained my friends. And, my "Something Extra," which I felt I needed as a stepping stone to higher ambition, enriched my life in other, unexpected ways. Our first year, we invited Don Barnette, one of the Harlem Globetrotters, to our camp, and he introduced us to the Athlete's Prayer. We had the boys recite it before every meal: breakfast, lunch, and dinner. At our Awards Ceremony at the end of camp, I gave each participant a copy, and I still have it hanging on the wall of my study.

Throughout my career at Western, at the beginning of each game, wherever we went, we put our hands together in the huddle and said the prayer. Photographers wanted to stage a photo of our team saying the prayer, and I never allowed it. To me, it wasn't a publicity thing; it was a solemn shared moment to help get us ready to play.

THE RED COAT AND THE

GOLD WATCH

We don't often think about the effect our actions have on others, but when I saw the classic movie *It's a Wonderful Life,* I was reminded of an incident that happened my last year at Lind High School.

That summer, at school's end, the grade school principal, who was also a part-time teacher of the sixth grade, decided to take the kids on a special outing just west of Spokane. I was also teaching sixth grade part-time so I went on the bus with them. We were going to have a picnic by the Spokane River. Now, at this particular spot, and especially in late spring, the river ran very fast there. This was on an Indian reservation, and there was a chute leading into the river where the Indians would throw their garbage and the rapid current would carry it downriver. I had grown up on that river and had swum there many times.

I was eating my lunch up on a knoll when one of the sixth grade girls, Virginia Richie, came up to tell me that Steve Sackmann had fallen in the river. She seemed pretty calm, not excited at all, so I figured he had just gotten his feet wet. I almost didn't bother to get up. But then something told me I'd better go look. When I got to the water's edge, I saw Steve, now about fifteen yards away, flailing about, and bobbing up and down. I dove in, but by the time I got to the spot where I thought he was, I couldn't find him. I guessed he had gone to the bottom. I looked down and peered around. I saw a red coat on the bottom beneath me. I duck dove down and grabbed it, pulling Steve back up to the surface. I was trying to get us back to shore but the eddy was too swift and kept pushing us out and around. Everybody was standing and watching but nobody helped us; as we got closer to shore, the eddy pulled us out and around again. We had about a forty-yard ride I imagine!

The second time we got close to shore, people grabbed Steve feet first and pulled him up on the steep bank with his head down close to the water. I think that was what saved him because, as I stood in the water giving him artificial respiration, the water came gushing out. I did it several times, and finally no more water came out; he started breathing again. They took Steve to a nearby home and gave him a bath.

The principal didn't want anyone to know about the incident as he knew he'd be in trouble if anyone found out he had taken the group there. No one ever mentioned it again, but several months later, after we had moved to Bellingham for my new coaching job at Western, I received a package from Steve Sackmann's dad. Steve had taken him to the spot where he had fallen in and almost drowned. In the package was a "thank you" gold watch.

That fall, since he didn't have a watch of his own, I let my son Jeff wear my gold watch so he would come home on time from duck hunting. That was Jeff's favorite pastime. He would shoot a duck out over the lake, and the duck would land in the water. Then Jeff would have his dog go out to retrieve the duck. Well, this one time, the dog wouldn't go so Jeff decided to throw a stick out in the lake so the dog would go fetch it and/or the duck. The stick went flying, but so did my watch!

A few years ago, Doris and I were visiting one of my former high school classmates, Elsie Meenach. She and her husband Ray had become wonderful friends; we had lived with them when I coached at Freeman. Elsie told me that her granddaughter, Jamie, was engaged to a young man named Jeff, whose uncle, Steve Sackmann, had been saved from drowning when he was a child. On a visit to Steve's home, Jamie had been shown a red coat that they had kept because it had saved his life.

So even though the gold watch is lying somewhere in the bottom of Lake Samish, I'm happy the red coat is still around as a reminder of a very eventful day in both our lives.

SPIT TO WIN

While I was in high school, I already knew I definitely wanted to become a coach, so I started going to coaches' clinics. Now, trying to remember what I learned back then is difficult. I do remember going to a Washington State College (now Washington State University) coaching clinic where its baseball coach, Buck Bailey – who was quite famous – told us that when you spit, you need to spit to win. This has stuck with me through the years. It was his way of illustrating how competitiveness is major, no matter what the action.

Washington State University has had probably the best line of coaches as any university in our country. In baseball, it was Buck Bailey and Bobo Brayton; in basketball, Jack Friel, Marv Harshman, and Judd Heathcote, an assistant to Marv, who coached a national champion at Michigan

State. Tony Bennett, who followed in his father Dick's foot-steps as coach at WSU, was in demand by just about every university, even at a wage of nearly a million dollars a year. By the way, the current WSU athletic director, Jim Sterk, played for me at Western. I think getting such good defensive coaches as Tony and his father might just show a little chip off the ol' Western basketball program.

Another clinic I remember that was so outstanding was given by a coach by the name of Charles Lappenbush. Lappy, as he was called, was a football coach at then Western Washington State College, and he left me with a real respect for both him and Western.

As I think back, I don't believe our university, including myself, ever gave Lappy the respect he deserved.

As for players, some of the greatest competitors ever at Western, I think, were athletes from my first year there. They were the most aggressive group I ever coached. Three of the players on that team are now in the Washington State Basketball Coaches Hall of Fame: Jim Adams, Don Huston, and Joe Richer. I have a feeling that Denny Huston will join that group someday. Our practices back then were like war, especially when Joe Richer and Don Huston were competing for the same position. You would think they were out to kill each other. Well, as with the whole team, when they left the gym floor and went to the shower room, they were best friends. In fact, Joe and Don ended up best man at each other's wedding.

Joe Richer was probably a step ahead of us all in commitment – he gave up coaching when he felt he was neglecting his family. I imagine most coaches feel torn between family and the demands of their sport. I know I did. Joe

Coach Chuck with Assistant Coach Joe Richer.

died at an early age. The message was clear: He had made the right decision as he was able to spend his last years with his family.

Jim Adams, too, did some wonderful things family-wise. He had a special-needs son so Jim not only coached, which is very time-consuming, but also took a night job to make extra money so he could send his son to a special school. His son really improved with the extra help.

Our team had two players who had to overcome some difficult problems. Denny Huston had what they called pronated hands. He had to catch the ball with the back of his hands. He also had diabetes.

Bob Thomas, another player on that team, had one glass eye. I tried covering up one eye to see how he played, and believe me, it is a lot harder than you might think. (Bob's reminiscences appear later in this book.)

It's amazing that this team could win like they did. When I got the job at Western, I tried to bring three great players with me from California. I know that if I had gotten them to go, along with the players we already had, we would have been the best team in the U.S. In fact, any one of them would have made us NAIA champions.

One of these was Keith Erickson. Before I had the job at Western, UCLA's John Wooden contacted me to get my opinion about another player. I told him that in my opinion he would do much better recruiting a player named Keith Erickson. But, it turned out that Keith didn't have a 3-point grade average, so John wasn't going to be able to take him. Besides, Keith's parents were moving to Seattle so Keith was ready to go to Western. Later, UCLA changed its ruling, and John was able to get a couple of players in under the 3.0 average. He immediately recruited Keith, which turned out to be a winner for both of them: Keith was a starter on John's first national championship team.

The second player I wanted was Clayborn Jones. As soon as I was told I had the Western job, I went to a gym looking for players. Both college players and pro players were there practicing. Well, right away one guy caught my eye. After seeing him block a shot and trap it against the backboard and, while still in the air throw a perfect pass the entire length of the gym for a lay in, I knew he had the talent I wanted. Clayborn's nickname was Cloudburst. Well, Cloudburst and I got along really well so he joined our basketball camp at Snow Valley as a counselor. He was anxious to enroll at Western, but as it turned out his grade point was 2.4, and at Western he needed a 2.5. They wouldn't accept him. He was very disappointed but ended up playing at Azusa Pacific University in California where he still holds most of the school records.

The third player I wanted was my best player from El Segundo High School – Andy Anderson. He might have been the best of the three. Andy was an only child; his dad was chief of police of Beverly Hills, a former FBI agent who had been second-in-command to J. Edgar Hoover. Andy's mom and dad were separated, and his mother wanted him to live at home so she wouldn't have to live alone. So Andy stayed with her while going to college at the University of Southern California. He did not play basketball there. He told Kirk Brown, one of his teammates, that he wouldn't play if he couldn't play for me. Although that showed how loyal and dedicated players can be to a coach, I wish he wouldn't have done that because he held a lot of promise.

Putting all of these things together, I will end this chapter by saying that every great coach or player I have ever known has been an exceptional, aggressive competitor but also has displayed special care for other people. This attention to others plays a major part in their success.

So, when you spit, spit to win – but not into the wind!

LIFE AT WESTERN

My career at Western was as satisfying as I had hoped it would be. As the baseball coach for four years, I directed the Vikings to two national tournament appearances in 1964 and 1965.

Basketball season, though, was always my favorite. But in my fifth year at Western, coaching the 1967-68 basketball team, I felt something was missing. Although we began the season by winning our first nine games, including the Cal-Aggie Tournament championship, and the players were hustling and playing well together, their effort still just seemed half-hearted.

This isn't to say that this team wasn't a group of outstanding individuals. In every other aspect – personal character, training discipline, enthusiasm – they were everything a coach could ask for. But, it seems to me, if you're going to participate in anything, you should put total effort into it from beginning to end. I could identify the problem all right, but I couldn't seem to think of a solution.

We went into the second half of the season and began our Evergreen Conference schedule. In the first four two-game league series, we swept one and split three.

Soon our overall record was 14-5, and of more consequence, we were 5-3 in league play. At that time a berth in NAIA District I playoffs was given only to the league champion, so our chances seemed slim as Central Washington University held a 7-1 mark. I felt our team figured it was all over.

The Sunday following our third league series split, I was at church and feeling really low. It seems whenever I feel that way I listen a little more carefully to what's going on.

During the service, Margie Stoner, the daughter of a music professor at Western and a close friend, sang a song entitled "The Impossible Dream" from *Man of La Mancha.*

I listened to the words, and they seemed to penetrate my soul. By the time Margie finished, I knew our team could go all the way; all we had to do was win our last four conference games.

But how could I convey that feeling to my team? I tried thinking of different ways to do it. Finally, I knew what to do. I invited Margie into the locker room prior to the game the next night and asked her to sing "The Impossible Dream" to the team. As she finished the song, I looked around, and I could see the change in each player's eyes. I knew they shared my belief that we were going all the way.

That evening, we went out and defeated the touring Korean National team 85-76.

Western's 1965 Evco-Pacific Coast Champions

Viking Baseball

VARSITY TEAM—1st row: D. Hemion, Keeney, Smith, Larson, Caderette, Clayton.
2nd row: J. Dahl, Monk, Reed, Reiersgard, Jones, W. Hemion, Sherburne.

Manager—ERIC ZIEGLER   Coach—CHUCK RANDALL   Assistant—MIKE DAHL

1968 - 1969
WESTERN WASHINGTON STATE COLLEGE

Viking Basketball

Two days later, we beat a tough University of Puget Sound squad 78-75, and then we took two league wins from Eastern Washington State College, 79-68 and 104-66.

It was a brand-new ball club that played those games – a team with real heart and soul. They were together, hustling and diving on loose balls from the opening tipoff to the final buzzer.

Our final two games of the season were against Central Washington at Ellensburg. The Wildcats had an 8-2 conference record, compared to our 7-3 mark. We had to win both games.

During practice that week, Mike Clayton, one of my starting guards, developed a calcium deposit in his left thigh and was lost for the season. Nevertheless, we still felt we could win.

The first game was a struggle, and at the half we trailed by a point. In the second half, Central got momentum and, with the strategic use of a stall, broke the contest open and won 80-64. Our bid had come to an end.

Seeing my ball club lose that game was almost too much to stomach. I compared it to a toddler who, having just learned to walk, wandered out into traffic. Suddenly, basketball wasn't enjoyable anymore. I didn't want to coach any longer. I didn't want to do anything. But I also knew we had to play another game the next night. I couldn't just quit. I had to finish the season. The next afternoon, I called a team meeting. I tried to get them "psyched up" by explaining that no matter how badly we felt, we had to come back. That last game had to be a great one.

As I watched the pre-game warm-up that evening, I knew my talk hadn't been very effective. The team was somewhat "up," but in basketball that isn't good enough.

I couldn't think of anything else to do to help the situation. Then, just as I was walking to the locker room to give final instructions, Dave Pederson, a member of our junior varsity team, came over to me. "Coach, can we say something to the varsity?"

"Sure," I said.

With Pederson the lead-off spokesperson, the JVs proceeded to tell the varsity how much each of them meant to the younger team. One mentioned how Mike Dahl had helped him find a place to live. Another how Gary Reiersgard had helped several of them with their studies. How Rich Tucker provided inspiration, and so on. They even said nice things about me. I could feel the heart and soul returning to the ball club.

After all the JVs were finished, I asked them to join us in the "Athlete's Prayer." We all got together in a circle, some players kneeling, others standing over, our hands together in the middle, and said the prayer. When we finished, nobody let go. I was afraid to look up because I had tears in my eyes. But when I did, I saw that every man there was crying.

Well, there was no doubt in my mind that I wanted to coach. There was no doubt in my mind that that was one of the greatest moments of my life. All of the wins that season could not hold a candle to the experience of that moment.

And, to me, that's what life is all about – it's what we should want in family, in school, in community, in our country, in the world. In every portion of our life, to put our hands together in loving care and concern.

Three weeks later, at our banquet, the team presented me with a plaque that read: "From your 'should-have' team." Of course, they had this inscribed because our goal of going to the NAIA national tournament had not been attained.

But I felt a much more elusive goal had been reached. Many feel that togetherness, heart and soul, and feelings strong enough to make men cry, are impossible to achieve. That's why I'll always remember that team of forty years ago as the one that made my impossible dream a reality.

LES HABEGGER

This falls under the category of "It Seemed like a Good Idea at the Time."

Early in my tenure at Western, we were getting ready to play the Seattle Pacific University Falcons which, under their coach, Les Habegger, had become a regional power on the court. Through the years, their teams have been outstanding. We were definite underdogs going in. *I* didn't even think we had much of a chance, so I decided to take Kirk Brown's idea and use a different strategy: Instead of having my men go out before the game and warm up on the court, I had them do their warm-up practice in the women's gym, out of sight.

When they announced our team, we bolted onto the court as always, amid loud cheers. (One of the cheers was rather rude – "What do you say when you see a bum on the street? Ha, Beggar!") I could tell by the look on Coach Habegger's face that he didn't like my "dirty trick" of warming up elsewhere. Nevertheless, both he and his team figured beating us would be a piece o' cake.

At the start of the game, instead of having our center jump ball, I had our little guard, Don Huston, jump. I knew where they would tip the ball, so we stole it and went for a lay in. We got an early 10-point lead. Gradually, the Falcons got back into the game, and at the end we were tied. But our team continued to hustle, and we won by one point!

Some of the fans were up to more dirty tricks. They found the scrawniest chicken I have ever seen, hung a sign around its neck with the word "Falcon" on it, and let it loose on the gym floor. Later, they deposited it inside the bus SPU players and coach used to travel to the game.

Since I hadn't broken any rules with my unusual tactic of warming up out of sight of everyone, I thought that would be the end of it. Then one day I got a few calls from the media informing me that Tex Winters, head basketball coach at the University of Washington, was leaving and had recommended that I be considered for his job. But then I also learned that Les Habegger and the UW athletic director were close friends. I wasn't totally surprised when I didn't get the offer.

Although I'm a great fan of high school and college basketball, I also enjoy doing "armchair" coaching of pro basketball. I always thought Bill Russell was a great player, but I didn't think much of his coaching the Seattle Super-Sonics. I called the owners in California to give them my unsolicited opinion. They directed me to the General Manager of the team, and I told him the same thing!

"So, if we were going to make a change, would you be interested in the coaching job?" he asked.

"I don't think professional players would follow my strict regimen of no drinking or smoking," I replied. "I think I should stick with college basketball."

When they asked me whom I might recommend, I said, "either Dean Nicholson or Les Habegger. They're two of the best college coaches around."

Lenny Wilkens was hired, and Les Habegger was hired as his assistant. The combination proved to be successful. With Les' intricate knowledge of coaching basketball and Lenny's personable style of handling players, they created the winningest team in Sonics history that was also fun to watch.

PET KANGAROO? I'M GAME!

In early 1968, our Western team was competing in a tournament in California, which we won. Shortly after we returned home, we received an invitation from the People to People organization to send a team to Asia to represent the United States. They offered to send me with my assistant coach, my wife, and ten players. Western Athletic Director Bill Tomaras was very supportive of the trip so we scheduled a three-week tour. This turned out to be a very eye-opening trip for all of us.

In Taiwan, for example, since Marv Ainsworth was there without his wife, our host, George Foo, invited us to dinner and kept sending in pretty girls to keep Marv company – presumably overnight! Marv kept declining the invitation.

In the Philippines, for our protection we had guards outside the houses where we stayed. They had a big screen around the basketball court, separating us from the crowd. When we asked why, they told us it was to protect us from flying beer bottles! The officiating was absolutely lousy there. One guy undercut one of our players, coming down on his back. He had to be helped off the floor. Still, the players were mostly friendly to us. We couldn't say that for the crowds, though, who were yelling "Yankee Go Home."

From there, we went to Australia, playing games in the north, then the south. At Inverell, we were invited to go on a kangaroo hunt. Our hosts would shoot them out of the back of the truck we were riding in. Well, one of their targets was a mother kangaroo and after they shot her they discovered a baby in her pouch. I felt so sorry for the baby that I took it and tried to keep it alive by giving it milk, but it died the same day. During halftime of our game the next day, I was presented with a healthy baby kangaroo as a gift. I thought that would be kind of a neat thing to bring back home so I smuggled it on the plane from Inverell to Sydney. Then, I got to thinking I'd better find out how to take care of a kangaroo once I had it home. So, at halftime during our next game, I phoned a vet to see what I needed for my new pet. He told me in no uncertain terms that it was illegal to have it in my possession, let alone take it out of the country. So, I took it to the local zoo.

He or she (not sure what it was) was probably happy at that turn of events as I would have been a poor replacement for its mother.

A footnote to this event: A few years later, a team from Australia came to Western for a game, and one of their players came up to me and said, "So you're the coach that smuggled the kangaroo out of Inverell!" Apparently, an article appeared in the local newspaper there the day after we flew back home. I can only imagine what the *Bellingham Herald* would have said if I'd actually brought it home!

My Impossible Dream

KANSAS CITY

During the summer of 1971, I should have been looking forward to the coming season at Western with great anticipation. Seven lettermen were returning from a team that had finished with a best-ever 20-6 record the year before. The group included four starters – 6'1" guard Mike Franza, 6'5" forward Lee Roy Shults, 6'7" center Rudy Thomas, and 6'5" forward Gary White. And, I had recruited the best community college player in the state, a 6'2" thirty-year-old guard named Tom Bradley. Tom had led his Walla Walla CC team to a second-place finish and was named the Most Valuable Player at the state CC tournament. Altogether, it was the most talented group of players I had ever had.

The Bellingham Herald   Saturday,

WWU's Mike Franza drives to the hoop as Eastern Washington players look on during the 19

'Big Blue of '72' tu

WWU honors team for the ages tonight

By KENT SHERWOOD
Special to the Herald

The echoes still hang gently in

(Top) WWU's Mike Franza drives to the hoop as Eastern Washington players look on during the 1972 district championship final.

(Right) A jubilant Coach Randall and his players celebrate one of the team's 26 victories during the 1971-72 season.

Still, I didn't feel very excited. Even though the squad had a fine record the previous year, it hadn't been a close-knit unit as some of my teams had been in the past.

It was at this time that I received a letter from Ray Ciszek, a former coach at Western, who was now working in Washington, D.C. He asked if I would be interested in going to Africa to coach a team that was attempting to qualify for the Olympic Games. I replied that I would be very interested.

Unfortunately, or so I felt at the time, the deal fell through. Another blessing in disguise.

At the start of the season, I decided to put the issue that was bothering me right to the team. I told them that the only way they could reach their full potential was to give themselves up to each other – trust and confidence in each other were just as important as their own personal skills.

One of my biggest problem players in that regard was Shults. He was a fine all-around ballplayer, but Lee Roy would often try to do everything himself, especially at the end of a close game.

Well, a few days before our first game, Lee Roy came to see me and said that I should check on his eligibility. It seems that he had played a few minutes in one game as a member of the Oregon State University freshman team, but had been injured in the contest, and did not participate the rest of the season. He wasn't sure if an appeal had been made at the time, and if it had, whether or not he had gotten his year of eligibility back.

We checked it out and found that there had been no appeal. Bill Tomaras, our athletic director, made an effort to get the matter reviewed by the NAIA, but we were doomed to failure from the start.

The penalty for using an ineligible player is forfeiture of all games he appeared in and possible probationary status for a period of time afterwards.

So Shults lost out on his final year of play because he didn't want the season jeopardized for the rest of the team. No one loved to play the game of basketball more than Lee Roy. It was the greatest sacrifice he could have made. This had a great effect on the team. They knew what Shults had given up, and they felt it was up to them to make some sacrifices as well. Lee Roy was replaced at forward by senior Roger Fuson.

The season began, and we won and won and won. In fact, we were victorious in our first twenty-one games.

What made the string even more incredible was the fact that we weren't such a powerhouse that we could blow our opponents off the court. Almost every game was a struggle, but these players were at their best under pressure.

I remember Bradley tipping the ball in for the winning basket with three seconds left in a 68-67 victory over the University of San Diego.

I can still see Chip Kohr, the worst free-throw shooter on the team, making two from the line in the final seconds of a 77-76 overtime win over the College of Great Falls (Montana).

It was really something to see these guys come together. Each had been a star in high school or community college or both, yet each had given up that status for this team.

As I told a reporter during the season, "If the world was like my basketball team, things would be in great shape – no

A team focused.

jealousy or prejudice, just people working together and giving to each other."

We finally were defeated 53-45 by Seattle Pacific University and ended the regular season with a 22-2 record, winning the Evergreen Conference championship and qualifying for the NAIA District I playoffs.

The best two-out-of-three-games playoff series was to be with Eastern Washington University, who had a 21-5 mark. The EWU Savages had given us our only other regular season loss, 69-68 in overtime at Cheney. We had beaten them earlier in the season on our home court at Sam Carver Gymnasium, 83-75, also in overtime.

In the series opener at Cheney, we lost 71-60. One more loss and our season would be over. About the only thing in our favor was the fact that the next game and the final one, if necessary, would be on our home court where we had not lost all season.

The second playoff game proved to be one of the most unbelievable games in which I've ever been involved. We never led throughout the whole game in regulation play and trailed 71-68 with less than a minute to go. Then White was fouled and made the first of two free throws, but missed the second. We came up with the rebound, and Kohr scored to tie it at 71-all. We were into overtime. With the momentum now in our favor, we went on to a 78-75 victory before a standing-room-only crowd of four thousand roaring fans.

The third and deciding game was almost anticlimactic as we won 76-68 to take the title and earn a berth in the NAIA national tournament at Kansas City, Missouri, for only the second time in the school's history. Both teams in

The 1972 Western men's basketball finished the season 26-4.

Photo courtesy of WWU

Western's best men's basketball team brings back memories

Twenty years ago, a veteran crew of Western Washington University men's basketball players provided Whatcom County with one of its most exciting seasons ever.

The "Big Blue of 1972" won Evergreen Conference and NAIA District 1 championships on the way to the quarterfinals of the national tournament.

The team will be honored at halftime of tonight's Western-Central Washington contest.

It was a season of magic and thrills — a season worth remembering. For a look back at the mightiest of Vikings teams, see Page D3.

Coach Chuck Randall's thoughts probably mirror the caption on his son John's shirt.

Photos By BILL TODD

Coach Randall with the "Big Blue of 1972" who won Evergreen Conference and NAIA District 1 championships on their way to the quarterfinals of the national tournament.

HOW CAN WE LOSE WHEN WE'RE SO SINCERE?

A pensive Coach Randall may be mirroring the thought on his son John's shirt.

the playoff series had identical point totals of 214 for the three games.

To me, the NAIA national tournament was the toughest in the nation. Thirty-two teams came together and battled for the championship, with the loser of each game being eliminated from further action in all but the semifinal contests.

Since we were seeded fourth at the tourney, we didn't have to worry about facing one of the favorites in the opening rounds. Nevertheless, Findlay College (Ohio) gave us a lot of problems though we hung on for a 67-63 win. The next day, we defeated a tough Northeastern Oklahoma State University squad 74-68.

Hundreds of telegrams from our fans back home flooded our mailboxes. We learned later that nearly everyone also tuned in the radio to hear how we were doing.

We made it to the quarter-finals, facing Gardner-Webb College (North Carolina). It was a classic confrontation of offense and defense. The Bulldogs were the highest-scoring team in the nation, averaging 110 points a game, while we ranked ninth in defense, allowing only 65 points per contest.

At the half, we led 46-45, but although we held them to only 36 points in the second half, we just seemed to run out of gas ourselves and lost 81-75.

Despite the loss, no one could erase the many great moments of the season, regarded as the best in the school's history.

In retrospect, I think if Shults had been able to play, we could have won the national championship, but had it not been for his sacrifice, we probably would not have made it to the tournament at all.

I was moved with pride when forward Roger Fuson summed it all up at our post-season banquet. Upon receiving the "Most Inspirational Player" award, he said: "We were really committed to each other, not just as ballplayers, but as individuals and human beings. No matter which five were on the floor playing – first team, second team, or a combination – the loudest rooters in the gym were the other five guys sitting on the bench."

It was a season I'll never forget. To me, the squad going to Kansas City represented all of my Western teams who had worked so hard and had come so close to reaching that goal.

In mid-August 2007, I learned that Bill Tomaras had just passed away. It brought back fond memories of his unwavering support of our basketball program. I looked up our win-loss record and discovered that while he was AD, we won 153 games and lost 70. After he left about 1972, our record was below 50 percent, so I attribute much of our success to Bill's support and encouragement.

TURNING POINT TIMES TWO

Winning a national crown is the dream of every coach, whether he or she is molding young players in Little League baseball or working with superstars in pro sports. I, too, wanted that for my Vikings. In the 1971-72 season, we had compiled a record of 26-4, sending us to the quarter-finals of the NAIA national tournament in Kansas City and close to our dream. Here we were again, almost to the district playoffs, with only a few games to go in our 1974-75 season.

I will always remember that season as the most painful but also one of the most wonderful of my life.

I felt that it would be a special year from the start because of six seniors – Dick Bissell, Jim Hotvet, Keith Lowry, Craig Nicholes, Bob Nicol, and Chuck Price. None of them was highly recruited out of high school, but each

Former team captains and assistants gather to honor Chuck at the annual banquet for the 1974-75 team.

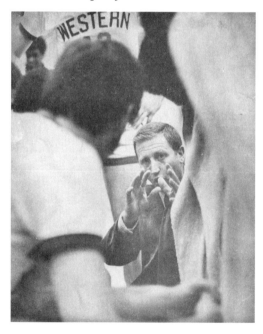

Coach drives home a point during a time-out.

had given everything he could to be a member of that varsity unit and have a successful season.

What made this even more significant were the obstacles all six had to overcome in the process.

Bissell, for example, did not play basketball during his first year of college.

Hotvet, only 6′3″, had played center as a prep and then had to make the difficult transition to a guard position in college.

Lowry had not been a member of the starting five in high school, but he worked harder than anyone I'd ever coached to become a starter at the college level.

Nicholes played in spite of the fact that he was 90 percent deaf.

Nicol, who had attended one of the State's smallest high schools, was only 5′8″ and weighed a mere 140 pounds, while Price had a speech impediment that nearly made him decide not to attend college at all.

Knowing the challenges they faced to improve, I wanted each of them to succeed not only as a team but as individuals as well. This made it even more difficult to make any coaching decision that might affect any of them adversely.

We began the season by winning seven of our first eight games, including a 76-75 overtime win over a strong University of Puget Sound team. Our only loss in that stretch also was in overtime, 77-73 to Pacific Lutheran University.

The whole squad was really playing together and was particularly tough on defense. In a game with St. Martin's College, we led at one time by a score of 52-10.

Then, we began to pick up some defeats along with our victories, which hurt us in our bid for an NAIA

District I playoff berth. With five games remaining, our record was 15-6.

A certain amount of tension started to envelop the ball club because we wanted to achieve that goal so badly. In one practice session, I noticed that the players were becoming somewhat critical of one another. The next day, at our team meeting, I brought up the situation, telling them that we would have to support each other to the fullest if we were to go all the way.

One of the examples I pointed out involved Lowry. Being an extremely sensitive person, Keith was hurt deeply by my remarks. During the turnout that followed, he was really low and the following day he did not come to the team meal before our game with Eastern Washington University.

But when the game started, Lowry was right there with the team. We had to win to remain in contention. He put on a spectacular display, scoring the last four points in a narrow 61-60 win over the Eagles.

After the game, Eastern's coach, Jerry Krause, asked me to come out to center court and look at the rims at both ends. It was obvious that one was level and the other was bent. You could see that from center court, but I had never noticed that before. At the end of that game, one of his players had shot the ball so that it had hit the backboard, then hit the front of the bent rim and bounced out. It was apparent to both of us that Eastern should have won the game. This started a thought germinating in my mind about the importance of rims being level.

The Monday after this wild, must-win game, I was walking across campus heading for the gym when I started

6'1" junior guard Scott Smith had been inherited from Ernie McKie's West Linn High (OR) team.

to feel a pain in my chest. At first I thought it was my ulcer acting up again. I had had chest pains before, but drinking milk always seemed to help. This time, though, it was different; the pain grew more intense. As I was in the locker room getting ready for my class, I told Coach Long, the Viking football coach, and Coach Wiseman, the tennis coach, about my symptoms. I said I needed some milk. I also said I thought I'd go ahead and take the class and go to the doctor afterwards. They told me they thought I should go right then. I took their advice and was glad I did.

Wiseman got his pickup and I lay down in it. I knew deep-down I needed to get to the hospital soon. When we got to St. Luke's, we were met by a doctor who later told me it was the most severe heart attack he had ever seen where the victim lived. I was immediately sent to the ICU where I remained for the next eighteen days.

At one point, I felt that I was right on the brink between life and death and could have gone either way. Loving life the way I do, I had always wondered what my reaction would be to death. I found that I was not afraid.

I was so totally out of it that I was not even aware that cards and letters, players and their families, and even fans of the team, were streaming nonstop into my hospital room. And, of course, my wonderful wife, Doris, never left my side, though I wasn't aware she was there. It was especially tough on her because her mother passed away suddenly while I was in the hospital.

I was sent home for more bedrest, and in the next weeks and months, I received hundreds of get-well letters and cards. They had a more rehabilitating effect on me than any medicine could have had.

Coach Randall at work.

One very special note came from Mike Dahl, who played for me in the late sixties and was also my assistant coach one season. His card didn't begin "Dear Coach" or "Coach Randall." It read:

> Randall –
> God loves you,
> And so do I.
>   – Dahl

It is still hanging in my bedroom.

By the time I was back on my feet, our basketball season was over. To my disappointment, we had only won one of the remaining four games. The losses came to some very tough opponents, but I felt I had let the team down.

This feeling was still with me when I attended our annual basketball banquet. It had been postponed until the first week of June because of my illness. The evening turned out to be a most special, unforgettable occasion.

Besides having my team and friends from the school and community there, also in attendance were nearly all of my team captains and assistant coaches from each of my thirteen years at Western.

It's a tradition at these gatherings to have each senior ballplayer give a short talk. Each of my six expressed his thoughts about his college career. I wasn't the only one there with a lump in my throat as I listened to them. One of the most moving was given by Chuck Price. Since his speech was hampered by severe stuttering, he had dreaded this moment. Yet that night, speaking to a crowd of nearly 125, his delivery was near-perfect. It was, I believe, a turning point for him.

Chuck Randall, Western Washington State College basketball coach stricken last winter with a heart attack, Wednesday became the 100th patient at St. Joseph Hospital to be served by special sophisticated cardiovascular equipment there. At left is Dr. Richard Schwindt, who heads a cardiopulmonary team which includes Kathy Macdonald and Jerry Smith (right). The equipment allows doctors to insert a tube into the heart, release a dye and take X-ray movies of the actual workings of the heart for diagnostic purposes. (Herald photo)

Chuck was the 100th patient at St. Joseph's Hospital in Bellingham to benefit from special sophisticated diagnostic cardiovascular equipment. Dr. Richard Schwindl (left) headed the cardiopulmonary team.

I realized then that the season had indeed been a success because it had produced six young men ready to meet life and whatever it had to offer. God made me realize that the love and prayers surrounding me had nothing to do with winning. I thought of how much God must love them and all the players I've coached. I love them too.

This helped me to prepare for the open-heart surgery I underwent two weeks later. Two days after my bypass, I was walking around the hospital and four days after that was discharged. I was mentally prepared to go back to coaching for the 1975-76 season, but when I found myself getting winded just walking up a flight of stairs, I thought I'd better listen to my doctors who told me not to go back to coaching just yet. Western hired a coach to a one-year contract – Jack Ecklund. Later, my doctor discovered that it was my medicine that caused my shortness of breath. Once I was off the medicine, the doctor gave me permission to resume coaching as long as I had a physical after each game.

During my time off, I rediscovered the joy of being with my family, golfing with friends, reading books I'd never had time to read, getting involved in church activities, and puttering around in my basement with more ideas for new inventions.

Still, I felt there was even more for me to do with my sport.

God had given me a second chance at life, and I intended to make the most of it.

THE SLAM-DUNK

ERA BEGINS

It seems that each new generation of kids growing up is challenged to run a mile faster, swing a golf club more accurately, kick a field goal farther. Whatever the sport, athletes push their bodies and minds to new limits to outdo their opponents.

When Dr. James Naismith invented the game of basketball, he surely didn't envision a player slam-dunking the ball. Heck, he just used a peach basket and a ball. He didn't realize how fragile the basket would become when some enthusiastic player raced toward the basket, and with two hands slammed the ball earthward through the hoop, causing the rim to bend and occasionally the glass backboard to shatter.

We didn't have any scholarship money at Western and the majority of the teams we played did, so they got first

Promotional brochure for the Slam-Dunk Rim™ shows Indiana University's Wayne Radford narrowly missing a stuff and appearing to destroy the goal, drawing gasps from the fans, but it was simply flipped back into place and the NABC East-West All-Star game continued.

A shattered backboard became a thing of the past with Randall's Slam-Dunk Rim.

choice on players. But this particular year, I recruited a player out of Oregon named Doug Creasey. He was fairly good size and could jump well, so he bent most of the rims. I had to keep going over to Bill Brown in the technology department to straighten them out. It would have been a major expense to completely replace those rims. What's more, our Vikings had even lost a game because of a technical foul whistled on Doug because he had hung on a rim.

My budget wasn't all that flush so, as they say, "necessity is the mother of invention." I needed something that would save a lot of time during a game, prevent potential injury to players, and help my anemic budget. And, as had been illustrated after a game with Eastern years before, it wasn't very fair to have some rims that were uneven on the court.

An idea came to me that summer while commercial fishing with my buddy, Ernie McKie. I knew that the propellers on boats have a shear pin so when the propeller would hit a rock or other hard object, it would shear the pin instead of breaking the propeller. I figured if we could put a bolt on the back part of the basketball rim, the impact would shear the bolt and not bend the rim. With the help of Bill Brown, I had found a workable solution.

My Slam-Dunk Rim™ (also known as the breakaway rim) gave way under as much as two hundred pounds of abuse. Two "pop bolts" at the top of the rim sheared off under excessive pressure. The lower portion of the rim was hinged to allow it to swing down without damage or injury to players. Replacing the bolts took just sixty seconds – if there was a ladder handy.

Allsop made six prototypes: four to go to pro teams, the Seattle SuperSonics and the Portland Trail Blazers, and two for our gym at Western. Ernie McKie, then basketball coach at West Linn High School in Oregon, helped me mail twenty-four thousand brochures to high school and college coaches throughout the nation. We also bought a full-page ad in a national sports magazine.

Another buddy, Marv Ainsworth, also helped us get the word out to schools. Athletic directors and coaches we knew would appreciate the cost factor: Instead of spending $25 to $30 to replace rims, they could spend just pennies replacing the bolts.

I'm a great one for bartering, so then I bought four motor homes in the middle of winter when they were less expensive, recruited eight students from Western, mostly athletes, and put two to each vehicle. I took a map of the United States, divided the nation into four quarters, and sent the kids out to high schools and colleges with samples and order forms. We paid the kids a little but not very much. (I guess it was enough that they didn't mind skipping a quarter to make the trip.) They returned at the end of spring quarter. This venture turned out to be fairly successful because I was able to get more for the motor homes than I had paid for them. I sold three and traded one for a lot in Sudden Valley, which I never even saw! I traded the lot for a trimaran sailboat, used it for a year or so; then I traded the trimaran for a condo in Mount Vernon, Washington, which I also never saw. A friend, Judge Moynihan, had a nice twenty-five-foot fiberglass sailboat I liked so I traded the condo for it. We enjoyed it for three years, and then I traded it for a nice anniversary ring for my wife. My trading days were over, at least for the time being.

But I digress!

(Top) Chuck demonstrates how easy it is to use the Slam-Dunk rim with its pop-back spring.

(Left) Chuck Randall and the second version of the Slam-Dunk Rim, which had to be thrown back into place.

As soon as I got the Slam-Dunk Rim going, I thought, "This is going to take over the world and make me a rich man." Neither happened! And, I realized the folks who build the better mousetrap would no doubt improve on my invention.

So, I went back to Bill Brown to develop a new design, using a ball-bearing spring principle, instead of the bolts. We put a hinge on the bottom of the rim where it attaches to the backboard. On the top was a latch held in place by a spring and ball-bearing mechanism. The spring tension could be adjusted to regulate the amount of force it would take to break the latch open and let the rim swing downward. It worked. (One of my former players recently told me, with a chuckle, that he still remembers having to push the rim back into place with a broom handle.)

Dean Nicholson, head basketball coach at Central Washington University, wrote me this letter after one of our games with the Wildcats: "The automatic recovery to their original position was very impressive, and the rims had the ability to withstand a lot of 'dunk' pressure....I congratulate you and give the rims my strongest recommendation."

The NBA proved to be a harder sell but they certainly saw the need. In an earlier game with Kansas City, Philadelphia 76er center Darryl Dawkins, known as "Dr. Dunk," had dunked the ball so hard that his 6'11", 251-pound mass literally exploded a backboard, showering the whole end of the court with safety glass.

An exec from the NBA called me and asked me to ship one of my collapsible rims to New York. Before it even got there, Dawkins broke another backboard, causing Commissioner Larry O'Brien to order him into his office where he imposed strict penalties for any further damage to backboards. (It took more than an hour in each instance to replace those shattered backboards.) They called me again and asked me to come back East for a test of the Slam-Dunk Rim.

But it was at the NAIA tournament in Kansas City that I was able to see it perform on national television. Someone else said he had come up with the same idea, which he produced for the so-called Toss-Back Rim Company. I learned later that one of the workers at the company, on hearing about my rim, was sent to see it work so they could copy it. The Toss-Back rim was installed at one end of the court and my Slam-Dunk Rim at the other. Though they were similar, it was later determined that I had the earlier patent and the right to market it. Paul Harvey even mentioned it in his commentary.

Now, I really expected my invention to make a lot of money, especially when such a popular maneuver as the Slam Dunk could now be used without all the damage and injury of the past. A major rim manufacturer in St. Louis turned out my product for a while but I wasn't really satisfied with the quality. I found a company closer to home that could produce as many as four hundred a month.

But, then, I thought about the direction I was going. Could I really see myself as a big entrepreneur, out marketing a product day in and day out? That might be exciting for a while. I had this other dream: My true excitement and joy were in coaching athletes. I wanted to get back to what I knew I was good at. I didn't need any other distractions.

I discussed this with my assistant coach, David Quall. David told me that his brother Joe was in business with a guy named John Simonseth of Everett, Washington, and that maybe they would be interested in marketing the rim for me. The rim retailed for $99.50. They agreed to handle the manufacture, production, distribution, and sales of the rim under their company, Basketball Products International, Inc., and pay me royalties quarterly – twelve dollars for each rim. Simonseth sent me a few royalty checks; then all of a sudden they stopped. I soon learned that he and Joe Quall had ended their business relationship. John assured me that nothing had changed as far as our business arrangement was concerned.

Simonseth knew he had a winner in the Slam-Dunk Rim so maybe that's where greed took over. When the checks stopped coming, I decided I'd better hire an attorney. I went to a large Seattle law firm recommended by McKie and explained my situation. Apparently the senior attorneys were too busy with other cases, and what's more, they charged one hundred dollars an hour. They assigned the case to a junior attorney, Kimberlee McDonald, who only charged seventy-five dollars an hour. I thought Simonseth would not renege on payments if they went through an attorney, so Kimberlee wrote a demand letter to him. She arranged to have the monies put into a trust account, from which the royalties would be sent to me by Ms. McDonald. McDonald had said the royalties would be paid until 1996 only and when I asked why, she said that at that time we would renegotiate. I thought that was odd but, again, I was too busy to focus on that.

All went well until the fall of 1990.

Records show that on October 17, 1990, McDonald deposited a check into the trust account from Basketball Products International, Inc. dated October 15, 1990, in the amount of $7,297.18, representing my royalty payments. McDonald then sent a check drawn on that account payable to me, for the same amount. It was dated November 1, 1990. The check was dishonored by the bank with a stamp ACCOUNT CLOSED.

I then called Ms. McDonald for an explanation and she said she would send the $7,297.18 to me from her personal account from another bank. It, too, was returned for Non-Sufficient Funds.

By now I was getting very frustrated and equally surprised at her conduct. I thought it was time I contacted another attorney – Andrew Peach of Bellingham. In March 1991, he filed a complaint with the Washington State Bar Association. A Disciplinary Counsel wrote to Ms. McDonald with the facts he had in hand, which would constitute "a misappropriation [of funds] in clear violation of the Rules of Professional Conduct." He invited her to respond to his letter.

The following month, April 1991, the Disciplinary Counsel wrote to inform me and my attorney that Ms. McDonald had filed a Chapter 7 bankruptcy in February and had me listed as a creditor. A meeting of creditors was scheduled for May 30, 1991. Andrew immediately sent a note to me asking me to contact the interim trustee who had been appointed to marshal the assets. I learned that because her taking my money constituted theft, this could not be discharged in bankruptcy.

In July, we heard from the Washington State Bar Association again; apparently, I was not the only party filing a complaint so a hearing was scheduled for February 12, 1992. It seems that thousands and thousands of dollars had been misappropriated by Ms. McDonald. She failed to answer the formal complaint that had been served on her. (In August 1991, I had received a letter of apology from Ms. McDonald, who had moved to Mt.Vernon, New York. She proposed to make payments each month, until the debt was repaid. She wrote again in late October, offering forty dollars per month. She never did make any payments. And when I tried to call her, her phone had been disconnected.)

In a letter dated April 8, 1992, from the Washington State Bar Association, I was informed that the Supreme Court had disbarred Kimberlee A. McDonald from the practice of law.

In 1996, I tried to locate McDonald to discuss our "renegotiation" and she was nowhere to be found. My attorney said that without her presence there was nothing more we could do.

But her troubles were just beginning: A trial was scheduled to begin on October 20, 1997. In State v. Kimberlee McDonald, she was convicted of four counts of first degree theft and two counts of second degree theft on March 6, 1998. She was sentenced to jail. Now, every three months or so, I get a check for about fifteen dollars. Whoopee!

I'm convinced that if Joe Quall and John Simonseth had remained in business together, none of this unfortunate stuff would have happened. Integrity walked out the door with Joe.

So, I guess in spite of my lack of meaningful revenue from my invention, I derive a lot of satisfaction from knowing that it has made a big difference in the sport and has brought the crowd-pleasing dunk back into the game.

Post-heart attack. Back to coaching.

FAMILY

Lauretta and Harvey Randall

My grandmother, Lauretta I. Randall, was an amazing woman. She was born June 17, 1865, toward the end of the Civil War, in the township of Moores, New York. One of my cousins, Dot, found Lauretta's father's name – Daniel Alan McConnell, on a census list in Ayr, Scotland. *His* parents had moved there from Wales, but when Daniel's chosen trade of carpentry was considered disgraceful for a person of his lineage, he left Scotland for America. He started a small carpentry business in the little town of Hemmingford, in Quebec. One home in need of furniture was owned by a Ahaz Asa Freeman, a lawyer, farmer, and sometimes teacher in Moores. Daniel married their daughter, Lauretta, grandma's namesake. They lived for a time in Hemmingford, but when the sixth child

*Lauretta and Reverend Harvey Randall pose for their 50th
wedding anniversary portrait.*

was born, my great-grandmother asked for a farm for her growing family, and he obliged. Meanwhile, the Freemans followed the rugged trail to newly opened territory "out west." They homesteaded and their descendants helped to establish the town of Rochester, New York, on that 160-acre homesteaded site.

Grandma met Grandpa Harvey when he was a young schoolteacher whose ambition was to enter the ministry. He accepted a position as a student missionary pastor in the pioneer North Dakota territory. They were married two years later, in December 1892, and settled in Edinburg, North Dakota. Grandma wrote a wonderful autobiography called *The Odyssey of a Great Grandmother*, which was printed and delivered in 1964 to her descendants by my two aunts, Olive Randall Reinstedt and Emma Randall Dasch. Aunt Emma corrected the errors and, with the help of Dot and her brother Phil, published it in 1981. It not only is a wonderful family history but also a glimpse of what life was like for those who married and raised families on the North Dakota prairie at the turn of the century.

Dot also found the following poem by Grandma among some genealogy material Dot had collected. Grandma had quite a gift for writings of all kinds but especially poetry, I think, and with more than a little sense of humor.

A Grandmother's Legacy

My Dear Grandchildren,

If you haven't done your very best,
*   and the sands of life run low,*
And your weary feet seem slipping o'er the brink,
And your busy hands are idle,
*   though your mind is active still,*
There's nothing left for you, but to listen and to think.

So, I'm thinking and thinking of the days that flitted past,
And wishing I had used them when they were within
*   my grasp,*
And grieving for this gift from God,
*   my talent, buried fast,*
Neglected for the duties <u>then</u>, that pressed me sore.

To resurrect that talent, I'm trying now to do,
But I see 'tis sadly tarnished by the years,
The napkin it was wrapped in is soiled and worn
*   and rent.*
Now I look upon the damage through my tears.

Soon my Master will be calling,
*   and my talent I must give,*
A talent lying idle all these years.
In penitent contrition,
*   that there's nought that I can do,*
I'll pray the Lord to pass it on to you.

(For a buried talent, see Matt. 25:14 and Luke 19:20)

Lauretta I. Randall

By the way, Grandpa Harvey performed our wedding ceremony and when Doris and I asked him what he charged he said, "Whatever you want to pay." We gave him twenty dollars, and then he said, "Oh, good, I'm glad you gave me so much so now we can give you a better wedding gift." And he handed the twenty dollars back to us.

Mom and Dad

My mother and I were very close, and losing her at such a young age was hard. From fourth grade to junior high, with no mom around to teach me, I had no polish, in fact no clean clothes. My nickname was Stinky! My dad was very distant and didn't seem to take pride in anything I did. That is, until, when I was a junior in high school and we beat North Central High. He seemed to take pride in that. He also was moved to tears when I left for the service so I knew he cared.

My dad remarried when I was thirteen and my stepmother, Katherine, was a fine woman. She set me on the right path and made sure I looked presentable at all times.

My sister **JEAN**, who now lives in Spokane and publishes a newspaper, sent me the following reminiscence of our dad:

I have a very distinct memory of our father: During the 1930s, when Roosevelt was running for office, Grandpa Randall, Uncle Willis, and our dad were very adamant that his promises would be a disaster for our country. Instead of going to local services for aid and finances, people would look to Washington, D.C. for answers.

I was so very impressed with their arguments I would sit on the floor in front of them and absorb it all. Our grandmother

Chuck's Dad,
Charles Sr.

Chuck's Step-Mom, Katherine.

Chuck with his dad, Charles Sr., and friend.

Sister Jean.   *Sister Joy.*

would interrupt with: "When you get together, can't you just enjoy yourselves?" I would think, they are enjoying themselves, and I enjoy it too!

Our dad would use our neighbor as an example: He did the chores for Dad when Dad had P.T.A. etc. evenings. Other neighbors also hired him for help. The community looked after him and his family without intruding.

When other people began receiving "aid," our neighbor's wife urged her husband to sign up. The first time he tried, he walked five or six miles. When the attendant suggested it was "charity," our neighbor walked out and walked back home.

She continued to urge so he finally did sign up. Soon he was no longer available for chores.

It was an example our dad used to point out what happens when the government interferes with local areas and their local responsibility.

I loved listening to them and realize how powerfully their discussions influenced my viewpoints on many subjects.

Another powerful memory: When I had completed my junior year in school, I was hired to help with house-work for a neighbor of one of our teachers. While iron-ing, I began to feel uncomfortable. It was determined I had appendicitis. I was taken to our relatives in Colfax for the surgery. The night our father was to come pick me up, my doctor-uncle said, "You know your mother is going to die!" No, I didn't! Mothers did NOT die! Our father came the next day; that Saturday night (on Sunday morning), our mother did die!

With my years as a parent, I have often thought about the pressure on our father at that time. He was teaching school, caring for our mother, and I piled on top of this with my surgery. I am amazed that it is only in retrospect that I appreciated what he was going through.

Doris and the Kids

DORIS deserves the credit for always being there for our three children; Jennifer, Jeff, and John, but I, nevertheless, took all of their concerns, trials and challenges to heart. I'm sure one of the regrets of any coach is the required time away from home and the distractions that keep us from focusing on family matters. I have so admired her strength through family sadness. Her older brother, Joseph Doran Reihl, was killed while serving in the Navy during World War II. He was manning an anti-aircraft gun during the raid of a Japanese plane on his ship at the battle of Leyte Gulf. When we went to the Philippines, we visited his gravesite. Her mother's passing while I was recovering from my heart attack, I'm sure, hit her hard. But Doris never complained and even today says, "It wasn't so bad. We've had a good life."

I love writing poems to her:

Doris, Doris, Queen of our estate
Thank God He made you my mate
Give praise to your father and mother in Heaven,
They made a great family, that means all seven.

*Daughter
Jennifer.*

Son John.

Your beauty is there for all to see,
    But your touch means the most to me.
You are now 77 ... [as] your 7 brings luck
    But you may not think so with your present
    from Chuck.

JENNIFER showed artistic talent early on. One of my most unforgettable memories is the time when, at age two, she decided to perform for us by dancing atop our kitchen table. I turned out all the lights and shone a flashlight on her so she would be in the "spotlight." A few minutes later there was a squeal and a thud as she fell off the table and broke her arm! She cried but the pain I felt was just as bad.

Our youngest son, **JOHN,** was diagnosed with schizophrenia when he was a sophomore in high school. It was such a heart-rending decision to send him away for a time.

I sent the following letter to him:

John,

Your mother and I love you very much. I want you to know that I have faith that you will put things together and become something that will help people, then you and I will both be proud of you.

I guess when a mother bird pushes a baby bird out of the nest it is hard on the mother and father bird as well as the young bird, but the young need to get away to learn how to make their way in the world. You have always been easy to teach, so I'm sure you will learn things well in Salem.

The Lord is with you and remember, we love you very much.

Love, Dad

And Doris wrote:

Oh, John, how sad I am to know that you can't be at home in the peace and glory of this beautiful earth that God has given us to live in. Yet I know that God will restore you to complete wholeness that you may reach out in love to others to share your life and the beauty that God is giving you. His great light of love is surrounding you. His presence is watching over you. His love is filling you. With peace and joy be renewed into wholeness of life.

JEFF struggled for a time with drugs and alcohol but he turned his life around and is a wonderful husband to Hideko and father to Novella, whom he named after my mom. We all live together, and it's a joy to have family with us every day.

Novella

One of my favorite pastimes used to be reading to Novella, my granddaughter. She especially wanted me to read again and again a story my mother had read to me and that I had read to my grade school students: Hans Christian Andersen's *Little Claus, Big Claus.* It so clearly illustrates how even a little guy can outsmart a big guy if he just uses his wit! Besides being a good artist, Novella enjoys writing essays like this one:

My Grandpa

Life with my grandpa is odd, although everything in my life is. I live in a house with three generations. That's pretty unusual nowadays. I have a family member for every hobby in my life. My grandpa taught me at a very

Son Jeff (#50).

Granddaughter Novella astride one of Chuck's garden "sculptures."

young age just one thing and that was basketball. Back then, practically his whole life was basketball, and he always wanted me as part of that. He taught me to love basketball, and he was a good coach, too, when I got older. Basketball became a big part of my life as well. I went to every game with him and was with him when he got his awards. As I was living in the basketball world, I knew all the players, thanks to grandpa.

But now I am eleven and things have changed. I now love to ride horses and basketball has been pushed aside. I still practice and of course I play, but it isn't the same as before. I go to about five games a year. Now, I'm always bugging my family to go ride with me. I will always remember that my favorite hobbies started with my grandpa. I used to ride at one of my grandpa's best friend's house. I know that whatever hobby I take up, grandpa will show an interest and want to be a part of it. That's why he is so special in my life.

That's all I will say about the family as I want to protect their privacy. Suffice it to say, they are one more reminder of how lucky I am.

Family Pets

As you probably have noticed by now, I love animals – even exotic ones. While I was teaching at Lindbergh High School, we had a donkey named Jenny, which the whole family dearly loved.

Maybe you didn't know it, but donkeys have a jealous streak. I found this out when I bought two goats. Well, Jenny just disappeared one day in November. We looked and looked but couldn't find her anywhere. There was a

Doris and Chuck still enjoy Christmas, especially helping the Fairhaven Lions Club with their annual Santa photo fundraising project.

nearby canyon where we assumed she went. A comment was heard on the radio during one of our games, "Randall Has Lost His Ass!" Two months went by and we had given up all hope of seeing her again. Then, one day in January, there was a huge blizzard, and when I came home from basketball practice, there was Jenny in our living room with my wife! Jenny was stubborn, but she wasn't stupid! She later gave birth to Dusty, and we eventually traded Jenny for a Shetland pony, one of my biggest regrets.

Jeff rides Jenny while Dusty tries to hide from the camera – or something!

POST-SEASON: BEGINNING

OF A NEW LIFE

In 1981, Western's administration refused to upgrade our basketball program so February 17 was my final game as coach. I was overwhelmed by the many displays of affection I received – from personal letters to banners and signs both inside the gym and outside. One sign on the Carver Gym wall read: "Basketball without Randall is like Bellingham without rain."

The following year, a close friend, Ray Meenach, who was chairman of the school board, asked me if I'd be interested in coaching the girls' basketball team at Freeman High. So back we went, this time as a volunteer coach. Doris and I stayed with the Meenachs during that year. Coaching the girls was somewhat easier than the boys as they seemed more focused. At the end of the year, I got some nice notes from them too.

An emotional Chuck Randall in his last WWU game as men's basketball coach.

When Randall and WWU parted ways, fans expressed their sentiments on a famous billboard boulder in Whatcom County (WA) just off Interstate 5.

More "Boulder Art" – this time for Doris.

One of them wrote:

Coach:

I really hate to see you go. I don't know what I will do next year without you....Thank you for all the pep talks before our games and for all the patience you kept with us throughout the season. I know you care for us all, and love us. I want you to know we all love and care a great deal for you also.

I'll always remember what you taught us: When I shoot for the stars and miss, I know I'll land on the moon.

Shawnell.

I still have many scrapbooks Doris has kept through the years with similar letters, Christmas greetings, and photographs of former players and coaches.

When I left Western, I was offered semiretirement, meaning I could teach just one quarter of P.E. and still make 70 percent of the salary I would make teaching the whole year. So that spring, I started recruiting student-athletes interested in going to Morelia, Mexico, in the fall. Our new experimental program was coordinated with Western's foreign studies program, then headed by Arthur Kimmel.

Students would stay with Mexican families during the nine-week session, studying Spanish in the morning and basketball in the afternoon. They could earn an average of sixteen credits, eight in Spanish and eight in P.E.

I thought a program such as this would really benefit basketball players who weren't quite ready for the varsity level but had aspirations of playing or coaching at the varsity level someday. It was also important for future Washington

State coaches to learn Spanish because it was the language spoken more than any other minority language here, so they might need to be able to communicate with Spanish-speaking players.

That summer, we drove to Morelia, capital of Michoacan, which lies halfway between Mexico City and Guadalajara. The head of the school there had arranged our play schedule. We weren't sure what we were going to face, and when the players came out on the court for warm-ups, you wouldn't think we had a chance. They were really good players! But when the games were underway, it soon became apparent that they were not disciplined at all. They would just run and shoot with no rebounding. We got all of *their* rebounds, and when we set up our offense and shot, if we missed the shot, we had three players there to rebound. In the opponents' wild kind of basketball, they had lots of turnovers. We won at least two-thirds of our games. The Mexicans loved to gamble on the games, but we didn't do any betting. It was quite an educational experience for all of us.

When we were ready to head home, our hosts gave me a parrot. I managed to get it over the border, but it wasn't long before I met someone who really wanted it so I traded it for a pickup!

One of our players, Dale Watson, had bought a beautiful ironwood carving for his mom. She decided to research its origins at the University of Washington and learned that it would one day be a collector's item. I was really taken with its beauty so when we went back to Morelia the next year, I bought some carvings too. On the way home, I stopped in Portland to visit my friend Ernie McKie. He wanted me

Former WWU men's basketball Coach Chuck Randall and his wife, Doris, have found life after coaching "isn't too bad." 3/10/85

Looking back, Doris and Chuck say "it was a good life."

10 WESTERN FRONT   TUESDAY, MAY 19, 1981

Sports

Espanol y basquetbol

by CURT SIMMONS

Anyone interested in learning Spanish and building basketball skills?

Chuck Randall of Western's physical education department and the former Viking head basketball coach wants the answer.

Randall said he is looking for 24 students, 12 men and 12 women, to accompany him to Morelia, Mexico, fall quarter as part of a new program sponsored by the physical education department. Randall said the program is on an "experimental" basis and is being run in coordination with Western's foreign studies program.

Students will study Spanish in the morning and basketball in the afternoon, Randall said. The basketball work consists of officiating, coaching and theory classes, along with clinics and "hopefully some exhibition games" with Mexican teams, he said.

Foreign Studies Director Arthur Kimmel said students will stay with Mexican families during the nine-week session. The cost, he said, will be $1,045, which does not include travel to Morelia or personal expenses. Kimmel said he does not expect the new tuition increases to affect the costs.

Kimmel added students can earn up to 18 credits, but the average would be about 16, eight in Spanish and eight in P.E. All the credits are transferable, he said.

Students interested in the new program must meet a few basic requirements, Kimmel said. They must have completed at least 30 college or university credit hours with a cumulative GPA of not less than 2.50. Students also must enroll for one language course while in Mexico and take at least 12 Western credits.

Kimmel said he thought the new program would be a definite benefit to both Western and Mexican students, although he admitted skepticism at first.

"I've never thought of P.E. as part of foreign studies, but after Chuck (Randall) proposed the idea, the more I thought, the more I could see the validity of such a program. I think it has real potential," he said.

The most important reason for the program is for future Washington state coaches to learn Spanish because it is spoken more than any other minority language in the state, Kimmel said. Coaches, he added, should be prepared to communicate with those students and players who speak Spanish.

Kimmel said he hopes the first-year program will continue if it proves successful.

"We hope to get a faculty exchange in P.E. someday," he said. "We can exchange a basketball or swimming instructor for a soccer instructor from Mexico. It's a great way for swapping techniques."

Randall said he thinks the program will benefit basketball players who are not quite ready for the varsity level but have aspirations of playing or coaching at the varsity level someday.

"And at the same time they can learn Spanish from the best program possible," Randall said. "And they'll have to learn a few words because they're living with a Mexican family. If they don't, they're not gonna make out."

The 24 students are subject to Randall's approval and anyone interested in the program should contact him before making any definite plans.

"If anyone's interested, I would like to talk to them and tell them more about it," Randall said.

"I think it's just a great idea. If I were a kid, I'd love to go," Randall said. "Heck, we'll have a blast."

Senor Carlos "Chuck" Randall

Señor Randall in Morelia, Mexico.

to show them to a friend of his who was a craftsman, and this gentleman told me how valuable they were, so I turned right around and drove back down to Mexico. This time I exchanged two thousand dollars which when converted to pesos doubled my money. I loaded up my station wagon with ironwood carvings and headed north again. On the way home, I stopped in art stores, museums – anyplace that looked like it might be able to sell them. Most bought them outright, but a shop in Carmel, California, took one on consignment. I think the owner put a price tag on it of about twelve hundred dollars. In fact, most of the places sold them for more than twice what I paid for them but it was still a good buy. I was able to pay for my entire trip with the sales. The following year, I stopped by the shop in Carmel to see if the piece had sold and discovered that it had been knocked over and was broken. I took it with me and when we returned to Mexico the next year, someone showed me how to repair it so the break wasn't even noticeable. From then on, breaking them didn't bother me; I now knew how to mend them.

The program in Morelia proved very successful so we went there eight years in a row. Besides good memories of our basketball experience there, I have beautiful mementoes in the form of ironwood carvings. Even today, I donate one each year to the Western Washington University fundraising auction.

One of the fun things I have been involved in since leaving coaching is helping the Western Women's basketball team fine-tune certain aspects of the game. One of the players wanted to know how to make hook shots so I helped her develop a successful technique. She became so

Coach Chuck goes over game strategy with Don Huston, his assistant.

More student displays of affection for Coach Randall.

Chuck sat on the bench at Western's Sam Carver Gym (above) for 18 years. These days, he's happy to work on another game – at Lake Padden Golf Course (inset).

good at it she stood out above all the rest on her team. So I dubbed her "my hooker." About the middle of the year, she came to me and said her dad asked her to tell me how much he appreciated my helping her but would I please stop calling her "my hooker." I obviously didn't know it had another meaning.

I try to attend as many Western basketball games as I can – both men's and women's – and still keep their stats. They graciously let me observe and offer my suggestions. They then do just the opposite, and it seems to work fine. I told them until they pay me to stay away, I'll be there! The coaches often ask me to run coaching classes, and I tell them they'll be surprised at what they'll remember years later. I'll never forget one of my coaches, Bill Everts, telling us that when showering, washing and drying between each of your toes is more important than washing and drying your whole body. He was trying to give us a visual image of the importance of attention to detail, and it has stuck in my memory. To me, it's just another example of the influence coaches have on their players and why I found it such a rewarding career.

Now, playing golf five times a week, getting together for bridge with friends, and puttering around my workshop seem to fill my days. I'm also trying to learn how to use this dang computer! I have frequent lunches with my dear friend, Paul Madison, Western's Sports Information Director, and other former coaches and players. They keep my memories alive. I am truly blessed.

Coaches and Captains
Reunion Time – with a great bunch of guys.

Ironwood entrepreneur.

EPILOGUE

I believe giving American teams the opportunity to play in sporting events in foreign countries is a very healthy thing for our world.

For example, our basketball coach at Western, Brad Jackson, took a group to China in August 2007 for the Elite Hoops International Basketball Camp, part of a TranSports tour, where U.S. high school athletes were able to practice and compete with their Chinese counterparts.

Brad's terrific wife, Debbie, shared his excitement in this mission. Her dad, Roland, a good friend of mine, is a former coach from Seattle Pacific University. I'm sure with Brad's background and knowledge, these clinics were accepted and appreciated.

At this writing, Brad and women's coach, Carmen Dolfo, have broken all records in Western's basketball program, with more wins and honors than anyone before them. So I have no doubt that one of them will be Coach of the Century for overall sports for *this* century. Lucky for me that I was in a different century!

I got to thinking about this. What a great program this is – sharing knowledge, skills, sports decorum, team building – on an international level; putting together clinics in all sports has gotten to be big-time.

The time we spent in Mexico, the Philippines, Australia, and Europe was healthy for all involved. Though we started out with just a mutual interest in basketball, it went way beyond that. We enjoyed getting to know each other on a personal level. What better way is there to get a greater understanding of each other's homeland?

Two of my former athletes – Ron Radliff (the Rat), whose dad was a coach, and Paul Hallgrimson – both outstanding guys, spent a good share of their life coaching abroad.

Ron went to Australia where he became a legend playing basketball.

Paul went to Europe, first as a player. Players were given various jobs to help earn extra money for food and lodging. Paul was given a job at a big department store to do displays. He did such a good job that he was asked to be in charge of displays at all of the stores in their chain.

Later, he returned as a coach and started an exchange program between high school players in the U.S. and Europe. While he was teaching at Sehome High School in Bellingham, he took a team to Europe, and Doris and I went along to help coach. We went to France, Germany, Switzerland, and the Netherlands. It was a great experience for both Doris and me. I'm sure Ron and Paul's efforts helped goodwill between the many nations we visited.

*More at home on a golf course than a dance floor, Chuck and
Doris nevertheless enjoy this rare opportunity.*

I love the Olympic Games for the same reason. As I watch them on TV, and especially when I attended the Games in 1968 when they were in Mexico City, I could see the good relations developing among the teams that were involved.

We are also finding out that a lot of these countries are developing some great players that are now being productive in the NBA.

This is a tiny globe we share and I often ponder a more serious "impossible dream": a world working as one unit. I think the shared love of sport is one of the paths to achieving this dream.

Meanwhile, I'll let my mind go back to golf. I have another new invention to help golfers.

By the way, I think I should tell you that I plan on being on the tour. The people I play with say NO WAY! But I tell them that about ten years from now they will have a Super, Super Senior for golfers over ninety, and I'm sure I'll make the cut.

Chuck (center) and golfing buddies took 2nd place in the 2nd division at the first annual Western Celebrity Golf Classic to benefit Viking athletics (June 3, 1988).

PART TWO

IN OTHER WORDS

Sadly, I've lost some really special people in my life. **Marv Ainsworth** and I were closer than brothers. We did everything together, played together in grade school and high school. We went to church every Sunday together and one Sunday he said, "Chuck, I'm the most Christian person going to this church." I said, "Oh, yeah? What makes you think that?" Marv replied, "Because there's envelopes on the back of the pew that say 'GIVE WEEKLY,' and I give *very* weakly!"

Marv was a superb basketball coach, both at University High and then at Whitworth College, where he was women's coach, also at Priest River and Valley Christian. He was inducted into the Washington State Basketball Coaches Hall of Fame. He was such a gentleman. He loved people but was a strict disciplinarian; that combination makes a good coach. We lost him to cancer much too soon. His wife was with him when he died and she told me his last words were, "It looks like I got the best of two worlds."

Still connected after all these years: Louise Ainsworth at Sandy Sinclair's homemade cabin.

Ernie McKie, my former partner, shared my enthusiasm for starting a basketball camp and really helped get if off the ground. He coached at Eastern Washington University and in West Linn, Oregon. He was a man who always stood by his principles and didn't hesitate to stand up for what he knew was right. I already mentioned the incident with the teacher when he was a student at Eastern. Later, when he became Eastern's coach after Red Reese, he stayed only one year, again because of what he felt was unfair treatment to him and his program.

Bill Tomaras, as I mentioned earlier, was an enthusiastic supporter of my Viking teams. As Western's Athletic Director, he was always behind me, so I probably should credit him with much of my success.

Instructors I had throughout school also left lasting impressions on me, some great, some not-so-great! One visiting instructor at WSC, Dr. House, told a story about a sixth grade boy who always got poor grades in English. The boy had really low esteem because he could never do well in class. Then, one day, on the way home, his teacher's car broke down and he couldn't get it started. As the boy was walking home, he saw the teacher and went over to see what was wrong with the car. The boy lifted the hood and right away knew what the problem was, fixed it, and went on his way. The sad part of the story is that the teacher thought, "That dumb boy fixed my car." And, the boy still felt like a failure. I think we all have things we're good at and should take pride in whatever gifts we have. Well, soon afterwards, Dr. House gave us a test and there were a lot of questions about our bodies' physical chemistry. I did very poorly on the test. I wrote on it that I really appreciated hearing his story about the "dumb" boy, because not only did I feel I wouldn't do well on the English test, I wouldn't have been able to fix the car either!

When I got my paper back, across the top in big red letters, Dr. House had written, VERY GOOD! And then below it, to the right, a little F!

That same summer, I was at the start of my Lindbergh High School coaching job. One of the seniors, Jack Blaine, had started playing basketball as a freshman but then was stricken with polio. Although he was still playing, I knew he wouldn't be a starter but he was coming along pretty well. I took him with me to college so we could work on his game during the week. One afternoon, as I was helping him, Dr. House wandered by the gym and started watching us. I had to go to class but Dr. House stayed and Jack told him what he was doing there. Dr. House must have liked hearing that story because from then on, I got A's on whatever I handed in and even an A as my final grade.

I think God gives us A's a lot of the time even when we screw up, if we show love and concern in our hearts. The letters and cards I continue to receive mean a whole lot more to me than House's A's ever did.

When I told my friends, former athletes, fellow-coaches, and anyone else who would listen that my friend Rose Brittain wanted me to write another book, I got a lot of encouragement as well as suggestions. Over the years, I've kept in touch with my "Basketball Brothers" and former players, and they recalled many wonderful times and experiences we shared. A few wanted to write a remembrance or two, which I welcomed. I had to do a bit of editing or this book would have been twice as long! I also wanted to include excerpts from some of the nice letters of recommendation I had. Here are a few:

From **Marv Harshman**, Head Basketball Coach, University of Washington (on my nomination to NAIA Hall of Fame):

I am writing this letter on behalf of Charles (Chuck) R. Randall whom I have known for about 25 years. I have been instrumental in helping him move up the ladder of coaching from junior high to high school to college. For 18 years, he was the head mentor at Western Washington University. It is one of the most highly academic orientated institutions in his district but one with little or no scholarship assistance. This precluded his getting some of the good players that other schools were able to get into their programs. I, therefore, think the results that he had over this period of time are much more important than had he been in an "athletic school."

The important thing about Chuck Randall is his dedication to the game of basketball. He not only was the first to start the modern idea of basketball camps in the State of Washington but also was a great innovator in attempting to improve the game, in any way possible.... He was the inventor of the basketball rim...the first and foremost of all collapsible type rims which everyone copied from his idea. ...

Chuck Randall epitomizes what we would say is the coaches' coach. He is a teacher, strategist, a counselor, and a father. He is someone we would like to have our sons duplicate and if at all possible play under him for a four-year program.

There are many people who make the Hall of Fame because they have the right amount of numbers. I think quite often we miss the boat and fail to recognize that there are people, by nature of their services to the sport they are involved in, particularly, to the people they deal with, that have made far greater contributions than just winning basketball games. For that reason, I would wholeheartedly endorse Chuck Randall as a most worthy candidate for the NAIA Basketball Hall of Fame.

From Western Washington University president **G. Robert Ross**:

It is a pleasure for me to write a letter of recommendation for Charles R. Randall for the NAIA Hall of Fame. Although I have been the President of Western Washington University for less than a year, Chuck Randall's reputation and abilities as a coach are already well known to me....Chuck's success goes far beyond statistics. Here at Western he is known as the "Coaches' Coach" because fully one-third of his players at Western went on to coach at schools (from elementary to major college level) throughout the Pacific Northwest. This speaks well for Chuck's love of basketball – he not only was able to inspire his players to perform well, but he left them with the desire and ability to coach others.

From **Dean Nicholson**, Head Basketball Coach at Central Washington University (a wonderful reference letter when I applied for a job):

"I have known and coached against Chuck Randall the past 17 years. Chuck built a winning basketball program under adverse conditions. He has had no full-time assistant, no scholarships, a limited budget, and a tough admission policy. In spite of this, his teams have always been competitive and well- coached. Chuck is a fine Christian gentleman and has always brought respect to the game of basketball and Western Washington University. Any father would be pleased to have a son play for Chuck Randall. I respect Chuck as a coach and as a man and give him my strongest recommendation possible."

From **Paul Madison**, Sports Information Director, Western Washington University (personal note):

Coach —

You have had more influence on my life than anyone else....I've never met a better human being and you and Doris will always be my role models for what true Christians should be.

You are the father I never had and having you standing with me is in reality having my dad there.

Thank you for your love and for your patience and for always being there for me.

Love, Paul

Sandy Sinclair, assistant coach at Republic, and one of the Basketball Brothers

I asked Sandy to tell the story of a trip he took down the Yukon River with one of his athletes. He included the whole adventure in his book *Striving* but I especially wanted to include his encounter with a moose. It just shows how far coaches will go to "build character" in their teams.

The salary [at Republic] was minimal, so we had to be very frugal to pay our rent, groceries and make ends meet. Though Republic was a gold mine town, it also had a saw-mill and the mill ends were hauled out of town by the dump so those with wood stoves could scrounge them up for free fuel. It was pretty degrading to see all the teachers bagging up wood scraps to save money, but I loved my job as coach. Marie loved staying at home just being a mother and coach's wife, though she was asked to use her new machine to wash the school football jerseys.

The year before we came, the athletic program was in sham-bles. They lost every contest in every sport, except one lone baseball game. The town had some rugged boys, but they had a tradition of drinking and generally poor citizenship. Before school started, Chuck and I took all the athletes for a three-day camp out. It was on the pretense of physical training but when we got them away from the negative influences, we laid out in no uncertain terms our introduc-tion to their "rite of passage into manhood." We advocated a selective pride in themselves, then used achievement in sports as the vehicle to gain that pride. Happily these rough cut mountain boys took to it well.

When my round ball coaching buddy Chuck decided to leave for greener pastures, I stayed on to coach my football team to become Tri-county Co-champions.

However, one of my quarterbacks was having a tough time getting along with his parents, contemplating running away from home, disregarding some of my training rules and generally being a teenage rebel. Yet I had a direct connection to Joe Bowe, as his coach. I felt the wilderness could be a salve to smooth over a troubled attitude, as it had worked for me, so I challenged him through my view of manhood!

Joe's grandfather, a town character named Major Bowe, had been on the Klondike Gold Rush back in 1898. I challenged Joe to become as good a man as the grandfather he admired. I longed for the Alaskan wilderness again myself, so I asked Joe if he would go with me on the old trail to the historic Klondike. I showed him a book of old Klondike photos and did some research on current status of that area. At that time no one had gone over Chilkoot Pass for years, as it had grown over and was considered lost as a usable trail. Joe accepted my challenge!

…Within an hour Joe saw two mountain sheep close to the river's edge, but we were too slow with the camera to get them on film. This incident precipitated a discussion about animals relating to people in the wilderness. I'd read in a book of fiction about a man who allegedly rode the back of a wild moose on a lake up in Maine. I'd mentioned that story to Joe earlier, questioning at the time whether it could actually be done or not.

Shortly after the encounter with the mountain sheep, as we sped passed a slough we saw a big cow moose and calf starting to enter the main river current. We turned around and headed back up stream to intercept her, but the current was way too strong for us. Not being able to keep even with it, we headed to shore for a close-up photo opportunity. Joe grabbed his 8 mm camera. I got the 16 mm movie and ran along the bank to where we thought they might come ashore, but they never arrived. It seemed we'd lost our chance. Then suddenly both the cow and calf came swimming in the current right beside our moored kayak. The current had been too strong for them so they couldn't get out onto the steep bank.

Joe clicked a quick close-up and then we ran back for our boat. We almost upset the food box as we jumped aboard to start our chase. The calf turned around and made it back to the shore he'd come. We caught up with the cow and I took off my shoes and dumped all the stuff out of my pockets. "Joe," I yelled, "Let's try to ride her rodeo style."

We came right up next to her but she made an evasive move that caused us to steer toward the downstream side of her. She then swam up stream so we would have to paddle like mad to even get close to her. We were both very tired from our futile attempts to chase her upstream. The cow was obviously leading us away from her calf. Why else would she let us get that close? After four attempts, we finally got near enough for me to try to leap on her back. I jumped but missed her saddle area and came off her back with only two hands full of moose hair. I then swam after my floating paddle and Joe maneuvered to pick me up out of that cold glacier-fed river.

It has been said that people can't survive in the Yukon more than 20 minutes because of the cold. I believe that. I got in the boat and we tried many times to get close to the moose again, but she out-maneuvered us each time, turning either upstream or downstream, whichever would be to her advantage. We couldn't get the middle of the boat next to her before she would turn away.

Joe wanted to try and ride her. After he unloaded his pockets and put on his life jacket I told him to look out for her front feet. The hoofs are her main weapons. He leaped but missed, yet I got a good picture of his attempt. I got him aboard and we went after her again. This time, however, the moose had reached shore and was walking out of the river onto a sand bar. We felt our show was over.

But again the current was too strong for her so she came back into the river to play with us some more. We got into position and Joe jumped again. This time he made it, but from the angle he landed on her, he knocked her over on her side. He couldn't keep his perch very long and fell off near her dangerous churning hoofs. He got kicked a few times but his worst shock was the flies, bugs and mosquitoes. When she went under water they all left the moose's head and adopted Joe. He about went crazy as a thousand buzzing creatures attack his head. He yelled, swatted, and finally ducked under the water to rid himself of them. Soon his paddle came floating by. I picked it up and we went chasing after her again.

I traded Joe spots to be up in the bow. The moose headed for shore, but by then we'd learned the art of the rodeo cutting horse. Joe and I worked as a team without words, each knowing what was expected and doing it automatically. This had been going on for half an hour. Mrs. Moose was showing signs of tiring, and we were nearly exhausted ourselves. Both of us were soaking wet and cold. The boat was a mess with three inches of water in the bilge, our cooking gear and mud all about. I put the 16 mm movie camera on the food box which was between Joe and me so we could both use it as needed. I wanted desperately to get that rodeo ride I'd envisioned from the fiction article I'd read. It now seemed almost possible.

We just kept after that moose until we saw our chance. I needed to climb way out on the bow to get that perfect angle to be able to jump squarely onto her back. Joe got the boat into the perfect position once, but my paddle got in the way and she turned away from us. Another lost chance! The thought crossed my mind that I'd blown my last chance. Because of that Joe had to circle all the way around her and it looked hopeless. He had to do it all alone as I was way up on the bow and not much help. Little by little, however, the boat inched into position. This time, when I leaped I made it all the way onto her rump. I got my balance and pulled myself into her saddle by grabbing moose hair. She immediately headed for shore and I whooped and hollered like a cowboy on a bronc. That is, until I looked down and saw her feet on solid ground. She was climbing out onto dry land where she was in control. At that point, I jumped off and swam after my paddle.

Sandy Sinclair, author of Striving.

"Basketball Wife" Marie Sinclair.

Unbeknownst to me, when I jumped for the moose, I knocked the camera from the food box. Joe grabbed it just as it was headed overboard. He caught it just in time, but grabbed it right on the lens, accidentally turning the F-stop down to the smallest opening. He told me later that he thought he'd captured all the action on film, but wasn't sure it would turn out knowing that the exposure had been cut down severely. Republic was a rodeo town and we'd never be able to tell this story back home, if we didn't have pictures to prove it.

The moose, seeing that we were not following her anymore, went to the nearest shore and just stood there and watched us. While thankful for the reprieve, she may have been thinking, "What manner of creatures are those?" I'm sure she thought during the chase, she had given up her life for her calf's freedom, because she'd used herself as a decoy allowing the calf to escape from these predators. We immediately picked the nearest place to stop and built a fire to warm up. Our boat was a mess and all our gear was wet, but we were happy river cowboys.

The sun was out to warm us as we stripped down to change our soaked clothing. It was lucky that our blood brothers of the Yukon didn't find us. We cleaned up, cooked a meal and ate yet all the while that moose just stood across the river and stared at us. Just after we cleaned our dinner dishes she suddenly took off to locate her calf that we knew was safe upriver waiting for her.

Joe asked me "OK, Coach, What do you want to do that we haven't already done?"

♠   ♠   ♠

Del Muse, another one of my Basketball Brothers, recalls the early days and style of playing:

If the historians are right, 1938 was the first year for the one-handed set shot, and legend has it that Hank Luisetti of Stanford University was the first player to use it. It must have caught on fast, because they were using it at CV in the fall of 1942. I don't remember anyone at CV using a two-handed set shot. Also, many players began to use the one-handed set shot at the foul line, replacing the old underhanded, two-handed shot. In a few years almost everyone was shooting the one-handed foul shot. The last player that I saw using the underhand foul shot was pro player Rick Barry of the Golden State Warriors. He stuck with that shot and was the best free-throw shooter in the league, as I remember.

When I moved to Central Valley as a sophomore, I turned out for basketball, at the suggestion of a new friend, Quentin Clark. I played on the B squad as a sophomore, and was 11th or 12th man on the varsity my junior year, which was a pivotal year for basketball at CV. A new coach, Ray Thacker, had taken over the varsity in the fall of 1942, and by the winter of 1944, we were on the way to the state tournament, for the first time. My good friends Quentin, Chuck Randall and Marv Ainsworth were on that team. Quent was an emerging star. I was 12th man; so I stayed at home during state. We had gas rationing, and no one went except the first ten and the coaches.

The next year I had worked my way up to 7th man, so when we again went to state, I got to go. We didn't place either year, but that was the beginning of a long and successful coaching career for Ray Thacker. He went to state almost every year for the next 20 years or so, and he won one state championship and one second place. I don't remember the year, but CV was playing in the championship game, against a highly favored school from the Seattle area. The other team was ahead by one point, with seconds remaining, when a CV player stole the ball and broke for the basket. The referee blew the whistle and stopped the play; then the ref said he had blown an inadvertent whistle. He then gave the ball back to CV, but they couldn't score with just a few seconds to go. Everyone from CV was sure that the ref had blown the whistle on purpose, so that the Seattle area team would win. Who knows?

My friend Sandy Sinclair was also on the basketball team, and he, Quentin, Chuck and Marv became lifelong friends. All five of us attended Eastern Washington University at least part of our college years, and we continued to play basketball, mostly in the Spokane YMCA league, during those years. Chuck was always the coach of those teams, and he also did all the organizing: getting a corporate sponsor, getting uniforms and arranging games. Quentin did have the experience of playing for a championship team at Eastern during his freshman year, along with another CV friend, Chic Sale. We added another friend, Ernie McKie, to our group at Eastern, and he and his wife Donna also became lifelong friends. Marv, Chuck and Ernie all became high school and/or college basketball coaches. Chuck was named Western Washington University Coach of the Century as we completed the twentieth century. The six men and the six wives have remained good friends since those days and we have seen each other frequently over the years. Sandy calls us the basketball brothers, and I guess that is a good description. Marv and Ernie are gone now, as is my Lois, but the rest of us keep going.

When I was a freshman at WSC in the fall of 1946, we had a player, whose name I can't remember, that still used the classic two-handed set. He was a good shot and played on the first five as I remember. Everyone else shot one handed. Also, Judd Heathcote shot a two-handed set, as a member of the freshman team, if I remember correctly. Judd had his own style, holding the ball at about forehead level and then pushing it up and out. He was quite accurate, but I never saw anyone else use that style.

WSC basketball was pretty good in those days, but not championship basketball. I remember that Vince Hansen, an All-American in the winter of 1945-46, sat out the 1946-47 year because all the veterans were coming back to school and he wasn't good enough to play up to Jack Friel's standards. During that year Vince would practice every-day, learning to catch the ball near the basket and take a short hook shot. He had a man checking him and a man throwing to him. They would do this time after time, try-ing to get him ready to play at a higher level. It worked, because the next year Vince came back and played on the varsity and did very well. He was deadly with that little, short hook.

Those 6'8" men in the 1940s were like the 7' giants in today's basketball world. They were the giants of those

Chuck, Del and Quentin – then and now.

Del Muse recalls some memories of the "Basketball Brothers" at his birthday party August 5, 2007.

Helping celebrate Del Muse's 80th.

Quentin Clark with two of the Basketball Wives: Molly Clark, Doris.

days. One of the reasons players such as Paul Lindeman (6'7" center) and Hansen were so successful and dominant was because of the narrow key. The free-throw lane was only six feet wide until 1951. Since then it has been 12 feet wide – a big difference. The old free throw lane was called the key, because it was shaped like a key. Big men could stand almost under the basket without violating the three-second rule, jump up and receive a high pass, and then take a short hook shot or a spinning lay up. The 12-foot lane stopped those easy short shots by the giants.

◢◣   ◢◣   ◢◣

I asked **Bob Thomas**, one of my players in the early '60s, to contribute his thoughts to this book and to be really honest about playing under me! Here are his memories, "dedicated to my teammates who checked out early – Keith Shugarts, Joey Richer, and Bill Zagelow. To the rest of us, it's overtime, so make the most of it."

We were raised in the era of Opie, the '50s, the age of innocence. We sat together in the Western Commons listening to President Kennedy commanding Russia to get the missiles out of Cuba. We watched as Vietnam grew from a minor conflict to a major war that would have a tremendous impact on our generation. We watched the Beatles come over from England and knew they could never play for Coach Chuck with that long hair. We were from small towns throughout Washington like Montesano, Camas, Sequim, and Sunnyside, and from larger schools in Spokane, Bremerton, and Bellingham. Yet, nothing had quite prepared us for Coach Randall and his brand of basketball and training rules.

The question reverberated around the laundry room, the site of employment where all the jocks worked for their scholarship money. "Have you met Coach Randall yet?" Since I hadn't, I was curious to hear the reactions of those who had. According to laundry room gossip, we would all be answering to "You dirty cob," while simultaneously being subjected to Sunday School philosophy. The rumor was floated that our diminutive coach spent his idle moments at church designing plays and developing philosophies of basketball based on Bible verses. I wasn't very happy to hear this as I was, and probably still am, the most irreverent player Coach Randall ever coached.

Our first meeting took place in Randall's little office at Sam Carver Gymnasium in the early fall of 1962. I was eager to find out if everything I had heard about him was true. I had played sparingly for Coach Jack Hubbard the previous year and had appreciated and enjoyed my relationship with him. In fact, we had shared a few beers at his going away party the previous spring. The first words out of Coach Randall's mouth dispelled any notions that I might, once again, be playing for what today is called a "player's coach."

"Do you smoke?" he barked.

I sat there flustered, not expecting anything quite so direct. My path was clear to me. I chose to lie.

"I used to smoke a little bit."

I fidgeted in an attempt to hide my embarrassment as well as my smokes. I continued fabricating. "I haven't for some time, however."

Damn, why would he ask me this question first thing? I spotted a list of names on his desk, one of which was mine. Right beside it, a comment was "might smoke." I thought, "Why would Coach Hubbard rat me out like that?" I remembered getting caught smoking by an assistant coach the previous year in Tacoma, when my friend and roomie, Jim Rife, got sent home for breaking team rules. I was told I'd better quit that nasty habit.

I survived the remainder of the interview as Coach Randall talked about his expectations for the team, which included going to the national playoffs every year. We had a good nucleus returning with Jim Adams and Mike Kirk being all-conference first team selections the previous year. It was easy to share Coach's optimism. Jim was everyone's choice for captain as he was as tough a player as there was in the league, and Mike could shoot the eyes out of the basket from anywhere inside 20 feet. I, on the other hand, was fond of the 25-foot range, long before the advent of the three-point arc, which, as a footnote, I'm sure would have increased my scoring and reduced the number of times Coach Randall cringed while watching me launch one from downtown.

Coach Randall then talked about being a defensive coach, and said that we would also lead the nation in scoring defense. I had played at Yakima Valley Junior College where our objective was to score 100 points a game, so we didn't worry too much about defense. I didn't realize at the time just how bad I was as a defensive ball player. That would become glaringly obvious in the weeks to come.

After 20 minutes of briefing about the expectations Coach had about training rules, I headed back to the laundry to continue my shift.

The laundry was our nerve center. Facts and fantasies were exchanged; pranks were plotted and parties planned. When I returned, I found that Bud Wienker and Gary Moore, two football players, had placed Ken Elvig, the laundry manager, in one of the dryers, and the mood in the room was one of stifled laughter. (It would become even worse the following year when Don Hagen took a dump in Elvig's lunch sack, and we all got fired pending the revelation of the guilty party. If DNA evidence had been a reality at that time, we all would have been sent downtown to give samples.)

The other basketball players and I talked about the possibility of having to change our ways with the new sheriff or, rather parson, in town. It couldn't be that bad, or that different, we decided. Jim and Mike had the good jobs given to the best players, working in the office at Carver Gym. There, they were privy to what was in the planning stages for the coming season. Little did we know what lay ahead.

As we were all gym rats, we played basketball every afternoon prior to the start of the season. Conference rules prohibited Coach Randall from doing any real coaching during these impromptu sessions but somehow, the little magician learned all of our weaknesses from those private workouts. He happily informed me that I was the worst defensive player he had ever seen, and that I might consider transferring to Seattle University where they were renowned for letting their man get around them, and then trying to block their shots from behind. As my leaping ability was easily my greatest athletic gift, I didn't see any problem with this. Understandably, with that philosophy, my defensive skills did not improve.

As the opening of the season approached, I was trying to get myself mentally prepared for some serious training issues. I figured I had better tie one on one last time before the season began. On a weekend that coincided with a football game with Whitworth, where a buddy, Gene Baker, was playing, we set up camp at the infamous Up and Up Tavern. It's amazing what you don't even hear or sense when you're guzzling beer inside a noisy tavern. As I stumbled out of the pub, the wind almost knocked me over. I had chosen a night for my final fling that would become known as the Columbus Day Storm – a night in which power lines were downed and trees uprooted across the Pacific Northwest.

The campus police did not treat me gently when they found me, and I was reported to Dean MacDonald for being out of my room and under the influence. Afterwards, the campus police manhandled me through the fallen trees to my room. Angered that I had been thus treated, I showed off the intellect that served me so well during my formative years – I left the dorm again. This great act of defiance landed me in serious trouble. Dean Mac set an appointment to meet with me on Monday to decide whether or not I would remain a student at Western.

After a sleepless weekend contemplating my impending doom, I entered the dean's office. Dean Mac listened to my story and my pleas not to be removed from basketball, and to withhold the whole incident of my transgressions from Coach Randall. I'll never forget his response.

"Mr. Thomas, I'm going to slap your wrist this time, but I guarantee you that if I have you in my office again, I'll hang your ass out to dry!"

To this day, I don't know if he told Coach Randall.

It would have been tough to tell. He was so demanding of us in normal circumstances that an increase in discipline or behavior modification could easily have gone undetected. Each Monday, after we loosened up and shot around, we would sit in the bleachers for a pre-practice meeting where we would learn about the conversations Coach had had with the Lord at church on Sunday, and what new innovations or inventions he might be working on. He would talk about the breakaway rim he was developing, or one of the million-dollar ideas he had. He always said that if he weren't dedicated to coaching young men to play basketball, he would make a fortune with inventions or ideas. The breakaway rim was one super idea, but moot for Western, since none of us could shatter a glass backboard, so his timing was okay from our viewpoint.

My defense hadn't improved very much; consequently, I was relegated to second team with Ted Liner, Joey Richer, Don Huston, Keith Shugarts, Gary Burch, Bill Zagelow, Dave Husby and Stan Bianchi. My nickname, Tom-eye- based on my last name and my one eye, was later nicked further until it became simply Toma.

The starters included Adams, Kirk, Bob Gilda, Denny Huston, and the fifth spot was wide open. I had a shot at it as did Denny Colacino, Joey, and Don.

Each day, Coach Randall taught us how to move our feet on defense by taking little steps, which resembled a form of tap dancing. Not only did we look silly doing this, tapping as rapidly as we could, but we felt silly. Our friends who dropped by to watch practice would ask us what in the hell we were doing, practicing basketball or getting ready for the winter ball. If I wanted to play, however, I would dance my ass off to whatever tune Chuck Randall requested. All that tap dancing led me to realize that not smoking or drinking just might be good for my stamina, as well as my health.

In the first game of Coach Randall's Western Washington career, we faced the University of British Columbia. I had improved enough to earn that fifth starting spot and be assigned to guard their leading scorer from the previous year. I probably had one of my best games of the year, shooting seven for eight from the field, blocking a shot from behind by pinning it against the backboard (Seattle University style), and shutting down their leading scorer. But the highlight, according to anyone who witnessed the game, came as I was dribbling the ball up court.

My glass eye popped out.

In the split second before it happened, I felt it dislodging, and was able to catch it in my hand and call time out. The ref came over to ask if I had lost a contact, and I looked up at him and said, "No, I lost the whole eye."

The look on his face and the laughter from my teammates and coaches will remain in my memory forever! Fortunately, the game is remembered fondly for a more important reason: Coach Randall, newly arrived via Lind High School in Eastern Washington and El Segundo High in Southern California, was 1 and 0 in his college coaching career. If I recall correctly, we went 3 and 0 in games during my career when my glass eye popped out – a record that will never be broken.

Until I was under the influence of Coach Randall, I would have been humiliated by this incident. I lost my eye when I was 14 as the result of a baseball accident. I was extremely self-conscious about my looks; skinny kid with the weird eye described me perfectly. This self-consciousness was with me up until the time I played ball for Coach Randall.

Coach Randall felt strongly that being self-conscious about a physical imperfection was not acceptable. They must be brought out and discussed so that everybody on the team knew and understood each handicap. We had so many handicaps on this team that in a speech he gave at a service club luncheon in Bellingham, he joked that our players were all graduates of the Buckley School (a state school for the physically disabled and/or mentally impaired). One by one, we discussed our weaknesses or problems.

These were unforgettable times at Western. And, 37 years later, as I was ending my educational career as a Principal at Sunnyside High School, I was nervously waiting for my retirement party to begin. To my utter delight, I found Coach Randall sitting at a table as my special surprise for the evening. I found it very difficult to control my emotions as I told how much Coach Chuck meant to me. He made me a much better person than I ever would have been without him. I know he has had the same effect on so many other young men who had the good fortune to play for him.

Western Washington University has achieved lofty heights in the basketball world because of the solid foundation laid down by Coach Randall. He continues his solid support – emotionally and financially – to the program. I know I can never thank him enough for what he meant to me.

📣   📣   📣

Denny Huston, one of my players on the first team I coached at Western, went on to be graduate assistant to Marv Harshman at Washington State University, then followed Marv to the University of Washington and was his assistant from 1971 to 1981. In 1981, he succeeded me at Western as head coach; then, the following year, he went to Wyoming as assistant coach for the next four years. After that came Stanford, 1986-88, under Mike Montgomery; and finally Denny became head coach at Weber State.

Chuck is one of the most incredible people I've ever met. The number of people he impacted is unbelievable. He loved being the underdog and he took a bunch of guys with little talent and kept telling us how good we were and we weren't smart enough to know otherwise! He said, "Individually, we can't do much, but there's nothing we cannot do as a team." He coached players to be coaches, telling us not just how to make plays but why. When we played Pacific Lutheran University, a winning team that we shouldn't even have had a chance against, we held them to only two field goals the whole first half!

Chuck is also an incredible innovator. For him to warm up the team in the girls' gym and not appear on the court until game time was a stroke of genius! They kept looking at the door, wondering where their opponent was. Then, when the Vikings appeared and we jumped at center to start the game, he had my brother Don, the shortest guy, jump against their 6'7" guy. Just these two acts, I believe, made our opponents mentally off-kilter.

Chuck was such a humble, unassuming guy, with maybe not as much polish as other coaches and certainly not the big school coaching experience behind him, so it's amazing to me that he was hired at Western. He must have had some really good interviewing skills or maybe they just saw in Chuck his incredible determination and heart for coaching.

He is also the most frugal guy I ever met. He never would spend any money on himself. At Western, our budget was so small that when we arrived in Las Vegas for a game, Chuck stood outside the airport and asked people who were getting into taxis if they would mind taking a couple of players with them into town in order to save money.

In recent years, Chuck has been beating himself up over not having spent more quality time with his kids when they were young. His kids love and appreciate him and always knew that basketball was central to their lives. I've told him time and time again that he had such a lasting impact on so many people that, unlike most dads, his influence went way beyond family.

Today, we get together as much as possible and at least chat by phone every week. Chuck is simply the best!

◀ ◀ ◀

Stan Kirschenmann is another lifelong friend I've known since my Lind High School days. He was a student there when we started the Conifer summer basketball camp at Snoqualmie Pass. In order to help pay his way to camp, Stan helped me with the promotion, mailing out brochures, and traveling with us to Montana to acquaint folks there with this new idea. He became a camp counselor and later took over Don Barnette's spot as a coach, teaching defense to the whole camp. Stan is a multitalented gentleman – a master at dribbling a basketball, a fine gospel singer, and a creator of magnificent, award-winning Christmas light displays at his home in Vancouver, Washington.

Chuck's 'can-do' attitude, I think, had a great impact on every young player he coached. I was basically a non-athlete, just 5'8" tall, but I was willing to learn and really wanted to go to the basketball camp. Chuck mentored me and helped me develop my skills. This really came to fruition later when the Harlem Clowns came to Western one year to play our redshirts. At that time, I was actually the announcer for the varsity games and junior varsity manager for Denny Huston, because both my knees had cartilage and I just couldn't play as intensely anymore. But, Don Barnette had taught me how to dribble showman-style at camp and I was pretty good at it. At camp, I did leg weights so I could jump high, listened to jazz, and lay out in the sun so I could get as dark as possible – I wanted to be just like Don Barnette!

Well, Al "Runt" Pullins, former owner of the Harlem Globe-trotters and one of the originals from 1927, had started this off-shoot group, the Harlem Clowns, but he no longer traveled with them. When he heard they were playing against us in Bellingham, he flew up from Los Angeles. Chuck came to me and said, "Why don't you perform while the Clowns are doing their 'magic circle' warm-ups to "Sweet Georgia Brown." This was always a familiar and favorite part of every Globetrotter appearance. I said I didn't want to ask Mr. Pullins so Chuck went over to ask him instead. Pullins agreed and said that would be fine; it would make the Clowns look even better in their pre-game warm-ups. So while they performed in their magic circle I put on my little show. It wasn't long before all eyes in the audience were on me, instead of the Clowns.

By the time I got back to the locker room, there was a message from Mr. Pullins offering me a job to do half-time shows on their tours and to teach his rookie players ball handling skills. I really didn't want to make that long-term commitment but I did follow them to Wenatchee, in eastern Washington, where I worked with the rookies for a day and put on a dribbling exhibition that night.

Since that time, I have worked with many players. I can still spin basketballs and teach. The camps, where it all started, were a great experience. I met John Wooden at Snow Valley and Chuck, also of smaller stature, was always fond of repeating Wooden's famous phrase: "It's not how tall you are, it's how tall you play." I met Bill Sharman of the Boston Celtics and taught his son who went on to Pepperdine College.

Chuck mentioned my annual Christmas displays. They are a real joy though we will be cutting back somewhat next year. They require two hundred hours of setup and I have help from six other guys. A few years ago, Sears sponsored a nationwide contest for the best Christmas displays. We had 30,000 lights, animation, Nativity scenes, a gazebo, a Bavarian village, and more. We sent in ten photographs and the required essay, which was written by my daughter. The phone rang one day with their spokesperson telling me we were a finalist. The next phone call informed us that we had won second place and the prize was five thousand dollars.

Even with all my extracurricular activities, including singing in a Gospel Men's Quartet, it's important for me to keep in touch with my amazing mentor of long ago – Chuck Randall. As it was with many of my fellow student-athletes, Chuck's genuine concern for me as an individual helped shape my future and deepen my faith.

Ed Monk was one of my early players too, who traveled with our Australasia tour. Sometimes it was a bit of a challenge to get Ed to listen to me. I remember one game especially where I did not like the way he played the whole first half. At halftime, I grabbed him by the jersey and said, "You know what, Ed? Five hundred years from now, this school may not be here. This gym may not be here. But *you'll* be here, because unless you start playing better, I'm going to kill you and bury you right here!" I think he got my point because he worked hard to improve.

I can honestly say I owe everything to Chuck Randall. I played basketball at Pomona High School in Southern California and we went to State the three years I was there. I was raised by a poor single mom and didn't really do well in school but I loved basketball. I had to earn money any way I could so I worked as night watchman at a juvenile detention home my freshman year of junior college. The 'home' happened to be right next to Azusa Pacific College. That's where I met Clayborn (Cloudburst) Jones, a gifted college hoop star. I'll never forget a night in June of 1966 when my friend Cloudburst told me about Western and Chuck and said he would call him and recommend me for the team. Chuck wanted some great black athletes like Cloudburst but CJ reassured him that I was a good player and "could jump out of the gym." Chuck said: "OK, send him up." I was beginning to think I would not get into a four-year college to play ball but Cloudburst and Coach Randall gave me a shot at a better life. A few days later, Chuck sent me the following letter:

Dear Ed:

A cloud burst told me that you were interested in attending Western Washington State College. We have a fine institution, an excellent academic program and a good Basketball program. I believe you already know about the NO SMOKING & DRINKING setup we have adopted here. As far as help financially we are on a need basis, which you should qualify for. I know your chances of getting more help will rest on your grades so keep your grades up.

Chuck Randall
BASKETBALL & BASEBALL COACH

Chuck was such an inspiration to all his players on so many levels but I, especially, felt he was the dad I never had. In June of 1993, I sent him the following letter:

Chuck,

HAPPY FATHER'S DAY!

Not having a father growing up, I think I gathered lessons and examples and guidance from whatever men were available to help me along the way. Just want you to know how valuable a father figure you were to me even when I was totally oblivious of it!

If a Cloudburst hadn't convinced you I could jump out of the gym, over the phone from Azusa Pacific, on a dark night in the spring of 1966, I cannot imagine who, where or what I might have become (probably lost in Viet Nam).

So thanks, Dad,, for putting up with me for a second (and third) chance, for the character-building, the tour to Asia/ Australia, the college degree, the summer job logging with Joe Zender and a chance to be a counselor at Conifer. I am so glad I met Thacker and Ernie McKie and Fred and Don and Dahl, and Riersgard and Jimmie, and all the other great male [role] models and friends. For an insecure kid from a dysfunctional home in California, it was the break of a lifetime.

Alice and I are enjoying the midpoint of our careers (about twelve years as special ed teachers). After an unstable youth, I am really appreciative of stability now. I think you and Doris modeled that for me, too.

QUICK TO PRACTISE

↑ AMERICAN basketballer Ed Monk, 23, sits amid a turmoil of luggage, but still gets in some practice after arriving in Melbourne yesterday. He is a member of the West Washington State College basketball team, the Vikings, now touring Australia. The team will play at the Albert Park basketball stadium tonight, tomorrow and Monday nights.

Ed Monk

I saw a bumper sticker yesterday; it read: "Good Happens"
It made me think of you, Coach. Happy Father's Day!

Love, Ed

I have so many memories, especially from the 'People to
People' trip to Australia and Asia. We were pretty success-
ful, considering the fact that we were from a small-town
college competing against players on the Taiwan, Philip-
pines, and Australia Olympic teams. One funny incident
happened when we were on national television playing the
Australians in Melbourne. My good friend Neal Larson
had a wisdom tooth coming in and had taken a pain pill
along with his fish dinner before starting the game. The
first time down the court he almost 'chucked the fish'. How-
ever, being a true Randall Viking, he knew "ya can't quit
on defense." Coach used to say: "You can't tie your shoes on
defense." So Neal waited until we got the ball back and
then exited the court with a mouthful of fish. When he
got back to the bench, Coach said: "What did you do, toss
your cookies?" Neal said, "Yeah, feeling better though." So
Coach said, "Caderette just got his third foul, so get back
in there." Neal feels to this day that this is a perfect testa-
ment to the Randall philosophy about defense. You never
quit or rest on defense. Neal knew he wasn't gonna run off
the course on defense, you fight to the bitter end on defense
and rest on offense. It worked – we beat the Aussies two out
of three games.

Marv Ainsworth got the nickname 'The Brake' on the trip
to Asia/Australia. Not because of his steady, kind personal-
ity but because at the hotels or in the locker room after the
games when some of us were getting revved up to go out

and meet some local beauties and party, Marv would come walking down the hall and say something like: "Hey guys, great game! So how 'bout we get a soda and talk it over and make some plans for tomorrow's game and then get to bed early?" Poof! There went the testosterone bubble and off we went to bed, safely guided by Marv's seemingly clueless guidance. He did his best to not seem a disciplinarian but his presence successfully put the 'brakes' on a number of (but unfortunately not all), ill-conceived adventures.

In Taiwan we beat the Taiwanese Olympic team four times and we were so well cared for that we felt like rock stars. I remember one day after practice walking back to our five-star hotel and hearing the sound of a basketball coming from one of the homes along the path. Four of us tall guys just walked up to the back fence and looked over. There were some young boys playing ball and when they saw our brown and white faces peering down at them over their six-foot-high fence they went bananas. A few minutes later we were all playing a pickup game with a bunch of kiddos whom we couldn't talk with but could easily share the knowledge and joy of this American game that had become the world's game. The kids' eyes went wide open as we slam dunked on their hoop and lifted them up to do the same. What a rush for these Chinese children and what a warm memory for us! The family managed to find a cousin who spoke English and the next day they held a huge barbecued chicken feast for the four of us. They couldn't believe how much food we put away and thinking back it must have been very expensive for this poor family. However, we got their entire extended family seats to the games, right behind one of the baskets and now we had our own private and *very enthusiastic rooting section of maybe twenty devoted fans. You can't buy memories like these!*

Oh, and then there was Coach getting on a uniform and bringing the ball down against a Taiwanese Olympic player. As he approached the top of our key, very closely guarded, he stopped and instantly hid the ball between his knees and pretended to snap-pass the ball past this poor young man's right ear. The guy turned around to see where the ball went while Coach grabbed the ball and threw it to an open player and we scored. This was possibly Taiwan's first introduction to Harlem Globetrotters-type exhibition ball. The crowd went into hysterics and Chuck just ran back down on defense patting the poor guy on the back and finally getting a smile out of him.

My first year at Western I played on the JV team and after one game Coach told me to keep my 'uni' on so I could get some varsity minutes as well. I was probably tired or over-pumped but I ended up spraining my ankle pretty good. After the game Chuck found me in the locker room on the verge of tears. It looked like I might miss out on the rest of the season (didn't happen, I was back in a week) and I was pretty down. He put an arm around my shoulder and gave that little chuckle of his (hmm, the 'Chuck chuckle') and said something like: "Monk, you played good out there tonight in both games. It's a tough break that you sprained your ankle but you'll be back in no time. Now get showered up, you're gonna be fine." Was that just a coach thing or was that also a dad thing? Felt like both to me at the time and that was pretty valuable for a guy who never had a father.

This father role wasn't reserved for me alone. Neal Larson relates how he and Tim Fikse (a JV forward) wanted to buy a house in Bellingham their sophomore year when they wanted to move off-campus. Banks generally don't give home loans to nineteen-year-old students so Neal and Tim asked Chuck to cosign for the loan. He immediately said: "Yeah, well, where do I sign? Just don't tell my wife about it!" We didn't realize what a big deal we were asking him to do. We were really asking a lot. They never did actually buy the house but it just shows the kind of guy he was and the trust he had in his players.

He was also protective of his players. In one home game one of our guys got injured and was bleeding and Coach tried to get the refs to stop the game. The refs didn't see him jumping up and down on the sidelines so he finally just went over to the scorekeeper and started hammering on the horn button. He got his time out, along with a technical foul, but at least he got his player out of the game.

I guess the thing I am most grateful for is the selfless, caring nature Chuck brought to our team, while still focusing on defense, hustle, and teamwork in the sport. He had no Kobe Bryants, nor did he want one. The hallmark of his coaching was sacrificing for the team and making sure everyone understood the value of being a good player, both on and off the court. One day I broke up a fight between two guards and Chuck later came up to me and said, "I'm proud of you for doing that, Monk." I don't think he realized what a meaningful affirmation that was for me. And, how that and other things he said helped shape me as an adult.

Tuesday, February 4, 1969

Ed Monk shoots hook over Carroll College defender, last Monday night. Western won 92-64. Getting in position to rebound are Mike Clayton (14) and Ron Caderette.

photo by seifert

Today, in retirement, Alice and I can look back on reward-ing teaching careers and we have Prasad (his name means 'Gift from God") our thirteen-year-old adopted son, from India. We are training for Triathlons and doing volun-teer work for Children's Hope International Foundation by raising $10,000 a year for YES! (Yatimoga Elementary School) in southeast India. Chuck and Doris modeled sta-bility in marriage which we feel we have had for the past twenty-eight years. Coach modeled clean living and love of athletics and both Chuck and Doris were always all about helping young people.

Doris was always this quiet but very strong and 'mirthful' presence in the background that always seemed to under-stand Chuck, especially, and all of us young hormone-driven guys as well. On the trip to Asia/Australia she was a rock and seemed to thoroughly enjoy every part of the adventure. Throughout his career, Chuck was so busy with coaching and on the road a lot, but Doris covered every-thing at home and was always a total support for her man and kids. I feel so lucky to have married Alice, a woman of strength and kindness who reminds me of Doris. Chuck and I are lucky men! We would not be where we are today if we had not been fortunate enough to meet and marry the gals we did! Slam dunk!

As I look back, in spite of being rather thick as a young man, it seems that I finally did 'get it,' Coach. So along with hundreds of other guys and gals whose lives were touched in your special way, I want to say: "Thanks for everything, Coach. You made a (BIG) difference!"

"Basketball Brothers" left to right, Quentin Clark, Del Muse,
Sandy Sinclair, Chuck Randall.

A celebration among octogenarians, friends forever.

Marv and Louise Ainsworth

Hall of Fame portrait.

I wish all of my coaches were still around so I could express what they meant to me as these wonderful players and colleagues have done for me. There is one, Bill Everts, whom I can still thank personally through this book. But I'll have to rely on God to relay my gratitude to Ray and Sig.

Chuck

APPENDIX A

Chuck Randall's WWU Players

(1962-'75, 1976-'81)

**Chuck Randall's WWU
Basketball Players
(1962-'75, 1976-'81)**

Jim Adams (1963)
George Asan (1964-65)
Jerry Ball (1964-65-66)
Dana Besecker (1971)
Stan Bianchi (1963-64-66)
Monte Birkle (1977-78)
Dick Bissell (1973-74-75)
Rich Blanc (1967-68)
Bryan Bloom (1980)
Mike Bohannon (1978-80)
Tom Bradley (1972)
Dick Brannon (1966)
Bruce Bravard (1980)

Pat Brewin (1965)
Terry Brower (1970-71)
Chris Brown (1974)
Kirk Brown (1965)
Roger Bruett (1963)
Greg Bruns (1980-81)
Kevin Bryant (1977-80)
Gary Buck (1981)
Dan Burch (1977)
Gary Burch (1964-65-66)
Don Burrell (1966-67)
Mike Buza (1972-73)
Ron Caderette (1969-70)
Bob Callahan (1975)
Roger Campbell (1973)
Doug Clark (1969)
Doug Clay (1979)

Mark Clay (1978-79)
Mike Clayton (1967-68-69-70)
Joe Clough (1975)
Denny Colacino (1963)
Doug Creasey (1977)
Scott Curran (1975)
Jim Dahl (1969)
Mike Dahl (1966-67-68)
Bob Delle (1967)
Mike Devine (1965)
Don Dirks (1966)
Steve Doerrer (1968-69-70)
Jim Dudley (1973)
Ron Durant (1980-81)
Craig Ericksen (1977)
Chuck Fisher (1972-73-74)
Bob Franks (1981)
Mike Franza (1970-71-72-73)
Brad Fuhrer (1975)
Roger Fuson (1969-70-71-72)
Hoyt Gier (1977)
Bob Gilda (1963)
Jamie Greene (1974)
Norm Gregory (1964-65)
Don Hagen (1964)
Paul Hallgrimson (1967-68)
Rick Harden (1966-67-68)
Dave Harding (1978-79)
Dave Hemion (1969-70)
Whit Hemion (1966-67-68-69)
Arnie Hendricks (1975)
Clayborne Henry (1981)
Oliver Henry (1981)
Tom Hilyard (1970)
Dennis Hill (1981)

Bob Hoefel (1974)
Jim Hotvet (1973-74-75)
John Hull (1964-65-66-67)
Dave Husby (1963)
Dennis Huston (1963)
Don Huston (1963-64-65)
Larry Jerdal (1964)
Danny Johnson (1970)
Jimmy Jones (1969)
Neil Kamphouse (1974)
Tom Keeney (1969-70)
Ken Kelley (1974)
Dennis King (1980-81)
Mike Kirk (1963)
Fred Knutsen (1978)
Chip Kohr (1970-71-72)
Kurt Langstraat (1981)
Ron Larsen (1966-67)
Neal Larson (1968-69-70-71)
Steve Laws (1973-74)
Bruce Lee (1977)
Jim Lee (1968)
Don Lehmen (1971)
Kevin Lindsay (1979)
Ted Liner (1963)
Keith Lowry (1973-74-75)
Bill Mahoney (1978-79)
Ron May (1978-79)
Bruce McClain (1978)
Rohn McCoy (1979-80)
John McCrossin (1981)
Bob McGinnis (1966-67)
Jim McPherson (1967)
Mike Merriman (1964)
Willie Miles (1979)

John Moham (1964)
Ed Monk (1967-68-69)
Tom Mount (1972-73)
Mark Murray (1974)
Dan Muscatell (1981)
Doug Nemo (1977)
Jack Nicholas (1974)
Craig Nicholes (1973-74-75)
Bob Nicol (1970-72-75)
Jack Nighbert (1965-66)
Ernie Olson (1965)
Dave Pederson (1968)
Pete Pilkey (1978)
Mike Preston (1971-72)
Chuck Price (1972-73-74-75)
Ron Radliff (1977-80)
John Reed (1968-69-70-71)
Gary Reiersgard (1965-67-
   68-69)
Joe Richer (1963-64-65)
Reggie Riddel (1975)
Mark Roberts (1970)
Al Russell (1965-66-67)
Bill Salisbury (1965)
Mark Salzman (1973)
Rob Scheibner (1979)
Tim Sheehan (1980)
Jeff Sherburne (1970)
Kent Sherwood (1973)
Keith Shugarts (1963-64-65)
Lee Roy Shults (1970-71)
Brian Skinner (1979)
Ted Slaeker (1979)
Ron Sloan (1981)
Ben Smith (1969-70-71)

Greg Smith (1977)
Scott Smith (1977-80)
Greg Snow (1981)
Jim Sterk (1975)
Scott Stetson (1970)
Ron Strandin (1977)
Jay Taylor (1968)
Mickey Taylor (1965-66)
Bob Thomas (1963-64)
Rudy Thomas (1971-72)
Rich Tucker (1965-67-68)
Dennis Upton (1980)
Rob Visser (1974-75)
Velko Vitalich (1977)
Herm Washington (1966)
Don Watkins (1980)
Dale Watson (1981)
Darcy Weisner (1980-81)
Gary White (1971-72)
Rick Wills (1981)
Vern Williams (1975)
Dave Wood (1975)
Dale Zender (1977)

**Chuck Randall's WWU
   Baseball Players**

George Asan
Gary Axtell
Arvell Bajema
Larry Belle
Don Berquist
Pat Brewin
Abbe Browne

Harley Buitenveld
Don Burrell
Sam Calles
Bill Fleener
Les Galley
Don Gard
Lynne Gillespie
Paul Hallgrimson
Duane Hammil
Don Harney
Max Hatch
Neil Hutchinson
Bill Jorgenson
Mike Kellogg
Russ Lee
Harry Leons
Warren Levenhagen
Chuck Lindberg
Clark Moore
Ken Moore
Bill Nelson
Jack Nighbert
Jerry Parker
Terry Parker
Bob Rae
Steve Richardson
Doug Ringenbach
Don Rosa
Alan Russell
Bill Salisbury
Bob Schwarz
Fred Shull
Ken Shultz
John Skov
Earl Small

Jim Smith
Robin Todosychuck
John Wells
Kim Wilson
Rollie Wilson
Gerry Yurovchak

Assistant Coaches

63-63   Ted Fromm
64-64   John Eckerson
65-65   Denny Huston
66-66   Fred Shull
67-67   Don Huston
68-68   Joe Richer
69-69   Mike Dahl
70-70   George Asan
71-71   Larry Stewart
72-72   Rich Tucker
73-73   Gary Burch
74-74   Bob Delle
75-75   Stan Bianchi
77-77   Galen Reimer, Tom
Lowery
78-78   Don Burrell, Kent
Sherwood
79-79   Dave Quall, Kelly
Heutink
80-80   Dave Quall, Kelly
Heutink
1980-81   Kelly Heutink

APPENDIX B

HONORS

In 1977, Bellingham Chamber of Commerce honored Chuck with Whatcom County Award of Courage for the Year.

NAIA Area I Basketball Coach of the Year   1972

NAIA District I Basketball Coach of the Year   1966, 1971, 1972

Evergreen Conference Basketball Coach of the Year   1966, 1971, 1972, 1975

Coached Evergreen Conference champion basketball teams in 1966, 1971, 1972, 1979

Coached NAIA District I champion basketball team in 1972, reaching quarterfinal round at NAIA national tournament; finished with school record of 26 wins and 4 losses

Coached Evergreen Conference champion baseball teams in 1964, 1965

Coached NAIA District I champion baseball teams in 1964, 1965

Coached NAIA Region I champion baseball teams in 1964, 1965

Coached baseball team to eighth-place finish at NAIA national tournament in 1964; fifth place in 1965

The Naismith Memorial Basketball Hall of Fame 1978

Western Washington University Athletics Hall of Fame 1981

NAIA Hall of Fame, 1985 (only the third basketball coach from the State of Washington so honored – after Leo Nicholson and Marv Harshman)

Dinner and Roast in Chuck Randall's Honor, 1989 (attended by over 200 former players, coaches)

Western Washington University Basketball Coach of the Century 1999

Western Washington University Overall Coach of the Century 1999

Western Washington University annual Thanksgiving Classic basketball tournament named for Chuck Randall, from 1998

Receiving Hall of Fame plaque.

INDEX

Photo Credits

Front cover, courtesy of *The Bellingham Herald*

Back cover, courtesy of Western Washington University

Courtesy of Randall Family Collection, pp. 4, 12, 15, 21, 23, 29, 35, 44, 49, 100, 101, 104, 112, 116, 117, 120, 123, 125, 126, 136, 139, 140, 144, 155, 160, 161, 184, 185

Courtesy of Western Washington University, Sports Information Office, pp. 10, 61, 67, 83, 85, 90, 95, 110, 128, 131, 133, 149, 182

Courtesy of Jack Carver, *The Bellingham Herald*, pp. 80, 85, 93, 97, 134

Courtesy of Ed Monk, p. 177